Y0-ARB-611

IMPERIAL BOUNDARY MAKING

The Diary of Captain Kelly and
the Sudan–Uganda Boundary
Commission of 1913

IMPERIAL BOUNDARY MAKING

The Diary of Captain Kelly and the Sudan–Uganda Boundary Commission of 1913

edited by
G. H. Blake

Published for THE BRITISH ACADEMY
By OXFORD UNIVERSITY PRESS

Oxford University Press, Walton Street, Oxford OX2 6DP

Oxford New York
Athens Auckland Bangkok Bombay
Calcutta Cape Town Dar es Salaam Delhi
Florence Hong Kong Istanbul Karachi
Kuala Lumpur Madras Madrid Melbourne
Mexico City Nairobi Paris Singapore
Taipei Tokyo Toronto

and associated companies in
Berlin Ibadan

British Library Cataloguing in Publication Data
Data available

ISBN 0-19-726154-X

Phototypeset by Intype London Ltd
Printed in Great Britain
on acid-free paper by
The Cromwell Press Limited
Melksham, Wiltshire

Contents

vi

List of Plates

The photographs and the captions are taken from Kelly's photograph album (Sudan Archive, Durham University, A63) and are reproduced by kind permission of Durham University Library.

List of Maps

Preface

Captain Kelly's diary is of considerable value as a contribution to international boundary studies. Kelly was born at the height of the age of imperialism when Britain and France were busy carving up the African continent and other parts of the world. By the time they had finished, over 80 per cent of Africa's land boundaries had been delimited by these two European powers. In general, imperial boundaries were drawn up with scant regard for the underlying human and physical geography and with little respect for the wishes of the people. The consequences of this process can be seen in the contemporary map of Africa, and they have been exhaustively examined in extensive literature by historians, geographers, and anthropologists. In Kelly's diary we catch a rare glimpse of how one such imperial boundary was actually created. It would be wrong to draw too many conclusions from what happened in the Sudan–Uganda delimitation since it represents the record of only a few weeks in the work of one Boundary Commission along a single boundary. To the extent that the Commission set out with explicit instructions not to divide tribes, it began with more enlightened objectives than many boundary-makers in those days. A combination of misfortunes, including shortages of food and water, and difficult vegetation and terrain meant that the Commission was unable to complete a thorough tribal and geographical survey. Crucially however the work was prejudiced by differences of personality and approach between Kelly and Tufnell, his Ugandan counterpart, which hampered their efforts to establish tribal boundaries. A major difference of opinion arose over Tufnell's readiness to punish uncooperative local people with force in spite of Governor General Wingate's express instructions to the contrary (FO 407/177 f. 48758 5 November 1912 (Public Record Office)). The Foreign Office also wanted the Commission's work to be kept quiet, and given very little publicity (FO 407/177 f. 2697 28 November 1912; FO 407/177 f. 27350 16 June 1913 (Public Record Office)).

There is however far more to Harry Kelly's diary than the record of an imperial Boundary Commission, however informative that may be. It also reveals many facets of African tribal life, and aspects of the everyday life of British colonial regiments over 80 years ago. Read in conjunction with Kelly's remarkable photographs, and with the exercise of some imagination, the whole expedition and the African landscape comes to life. The diary also reveals something of the character of its author although it is not primarily a personal document. Kelly probably kept his diary as the basis for despatches and reports to Wingate. Nevertheless Kelly's personality emerges from the pages and the readers can judge for themselves what kind of a man he was. Some will see him as the willing and uncompromising agent of his empire-building masters, who had no right to be interfering in the destinies of indigenous African peoples. Others will judge him more sympathetically, bearing in mind the values and attitudes of his day. In this context Captain Kelly may be seen as a man of considerable humanity who had greater respect for the African people than many of his contemporaries.

Acknowledgements

I wish to acknowledge my great debt to Lesley Forbes, formerly responsible for the Sudan Archive at Durham University, who introduced me to the Kelly papers, and suggested publication of the diary. Her successor Jane Hogan supported the project with equal enthusiasm and kindly corrected the final manuscript, deciphering a number of almost unreadable words. Thanks are also due to Durham University for granting permission to publish Kelly's diary and a selection of his photographs from the Sudan Archive. Figure 2 is reproduced by kind permission of the Public Record Office. The work would never have been completed without the indefatigable assistance of Elizabeth Pearson of the Geography Department at Durham University who first undertook the difficult task of transcribing Kelly's extremely puzzling handwriting. Patricia Toye undertook a search of the Foreign Office files in the Public Record Office for background papers in August 1994, a few weeks before her tragic death. I hope this book may be seen as a small tribute to her considerable contribution to scholarship through her skill and dedication as a professional archivist.

My daughters Carrie and Julia checked early versions of the text. In the later stages, Anna Oxbury, Margaret Bell and Julia Morgan of the International Boundaries Research Unit at Durham University undertook sterling work in correcting and editing the text time and time again. Many friends and colleagues also offered information and advice and I much appreciate their help and interest. They include Christopher Terrill, Dai Morgan, Lynette Mitchell and especially Professor Peter Holt whose prodigious knowledge of Sudan helped unlock a number of riddles in the diary. I also learnt a great deal from the scholarly publications of Professor James Barber of Durham University on British administration in Northern Uganda. Arthur Corner of the Cartographic Unit in the Department of Geography at Durham University drew the maps, and Michelle Johnson copied the photographs. Finally, I am most grateful to the British Academy for awarding a grant towards the cost of editing Captain Kelly's diary, and for James Rivington's patience while awaiting the manuscript.

Gerald Blake
Durham, July 1995

Introduction

Captain Kelly — the man

Harry Holdsworth Kelly was born in Southsea, England in 1880, the fourth son of Colonel H. H. Kelly. Educated at Rugby School he joined the army in 1899 and was commissioned in the Royal Engineers. He was a Fellow of the Royal Geographical Society. Standing 6′6″ tall he became heavyweight boxing champion of the army; by all accounts Kelly was a well known and extremely popular officer. In 1903 he was seconded to the Egyptian army and was appointed resident engineer for the construction of Port Sudan for which he was awarded the Fourth Class Osmania decoration (see Plate 1). In 1908 he was appointed Director of the Roads and Communications Section of the Public Works Department in Khartoum. Before being appointed Chief Commissioner of the Sudan–Uganda Boundary Commission in 1912 he had explored extensively in hitherto uncharted regions of South West Abyssinia (1908 and 1911) and the Sudan–Belgian Congo frontier (1910). He was an officer in the Beir patrol which conducted operations to suppress raiding by the Beir people between January and April 1912. Pibor post (Plate 19) was established in Beir territory following these operations (M. W. Daly, 1986; pp. 148–9). With this experience of expeditions, and his training as a field surveyor, Kelly was admirably qualified to head the Sudan–Uganda Commission. In November 1913 despite attempts by Wingate to keep him in Sudan, Kelly reverted to service in the British army. He was killed near Boisgrenier in France in the early stages of the first World War on 24th October 1914 while serving with 38th Field Company of the Royal Engineers.

Captain Kelly — the diary

Captain Kelly wrote a diary every day during the Boundary Commission which formed the basis for long and regular reports to General Sir Reginald Wingate, Governor General of Sudan. The diary is written in an army-issue foolscap size notebook with 104 pages. It was written in ink in a script which is at times extremely difficult to decipher, although mercifully Kelly took the precaution of writing names in capital letters (Plates 3, 6, 10, and 13). Nevertheless, six words proved quite impossible to read, and there was no choice but to indicate these by asterisks. Where there is some doubt, words are shown in square brackets. Inconsistencies in the spelling of certain place-names, types of grain, and names of people have been retained as in Kelly's text. The diary text reproduced in this volume covers the few days before the Commission assembled on January 15th 1913, and the subsequent expeditions until April 12th. There was almost certainly at least one other diary following this one recording details of Kelly's expedition to the Boma region to explore the Abyssinian frontier, but it has not been traced. However, this diary includes all the material he wrote during the Sudan–Uganda Boundary Commission. Used in conjunction with Kelly's reports to Wingate and his collection of 114 photographs covering his travels from the Nile to the Boma Plateau it is possible to put together a fairly detailed picture of the course of events. The diary, photographs, and reports to the Governor General of Sudan, Sir Reginald Wingate are all in the possession of the Sudan Archive at Durham University.

Besides the diary, Kelly must have kept a separate record of his field observations, and a map of prominent features in the border region. Both were almost certainly deposited with the Sudan Surveys Department in Khartoum. One has to admire the dedication of a man who not only travelled considerable distances in the African bush every day and carried responsibility for leading a large party of men and animals in a sometimes hostile environment, but who managed to keep such a fine record of events. Kelly's reports to Wingate give carefully edited details of the tribes, geographical features and the economy of the regions through which he passed. The Director of the Sudan Surveys Department (Hugh Pearson) who was clearly impressed with his work as surveyor on the Sudan–Uganda Commission wrote 'he has done a truly astonishing amount of mapping, far beyond what I thought would be possible' (Sudan Archive 186/3/102). He was without question a most conscientious and able officer, who might have reached high rank in the British army had he survived the First World War. Kelly's diary documents the role of individuals and the interplay of personalities in the evolution of the political map of the world. It is a reminder that too much attention can perhaps be given to great power politics in interpreting international boundary delimitations. In reality individuals had enormous influence in deciding the shape of the world political map.

Introduction

Political background to the Boundary Commission

During the closing decade of the nineteenth century British infl
was extending into a vast tract of Africa often known as Equa
This inaccessible and turbulent territory lay between the regions of
effective British administrations in Sudan and Uganda. British influence had become established in Sudan in 1896–99. Both France (in
1898 and 1899) and Belgium (in 1894) had recognised Sudan as a
British sphere of influence. The Uganda Protectorate was established
by Britain in 1894, and the administration of Uganda became the
responsibility of the Colonial Office. Sudan on the other hand was
jointly administered by Britain and Egypt and fell under the jurisdiction
of the Foreign Office. No clear boundary between the two administrations had been agreed, although Sir Harry Johnston, who had been
appointed Special Commissioner in Uganda in 1899, proposed a considerable northward expansion of what had hitherto been perceived as
Ugandan territory (Figure 1). Johnston had ambitious plans for the
development of Uganda, and he was determined to extend effective
administration into these largely unknown regions. Johnston's short
period as Special Commissioner ended in 1901 and Uganda never
succeeded in controlling the provinces and districts he had coveted. In
1902 however the northern limits of Uganda were indicated in general
terms by Order in Council as being those advocated by Johnston,
(Brownlie 1979).

Uncertainty about the precise delimitation of Sudanese and Ugandan
territory might have continued for many years but for the death of
King Leopold II of the Belgians in 1909. In 1894 Leopold had been
granted a lease of territory by Britain to the west of the river Nile in
return for his recognition of spheres of influence in East Africa agreed
between Britain and Germany in 1886 and 1890. This agreement, which
concerned a region usually referred to as the Lado enclave was to be
valid during the lifetime of Leopold. Thus when Leopold died in 1909
the territory was transferred from the Belgian Congo to the Anglo-
Egyptian Sudan. The transfer took place formally on June 16th 1910.
This created a large region of Sudanese territory to the west of Uganda,
extending as far south as Lake Albert, which could clearly be more
easily governed from Uganda. It was therefore decided to transfer the
southern part of the Lado enclave, as shown on Figure 1, to Uganda
in return for a portion of Northern Uganda, which would become part
of Sudan.

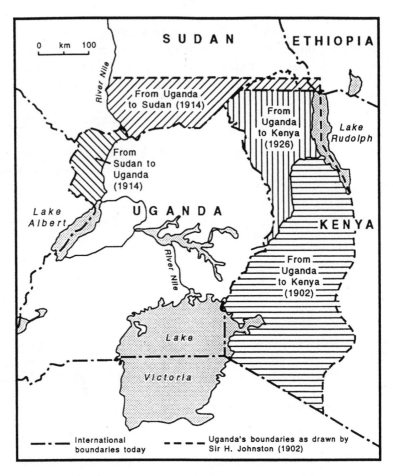

Figure 1. The political context of the Sudan–Uganda Boundary Commission in 1913

Apart from the obvious need to decide on the extent of the territory to be transferred, other factors were pressing upon the British to extend effective administration and control into Equatoria. Ivory poaching had brought considerable revenues to some tribes in the region, and these were being used to purchase firearms which were creating an increasingly unstable and hostile environment. Barber has given detailed descriptions of the problems of controlling northern Uganda and British attempts to extend effective administration. This instability partly explains the size of the escort which Kelly took with him on the

Commission. The territory to be visited by the Boundary Commission was inhabited by quarrelsome tribes with increasing access to firearms and ammunition. In northwest Uganda in the Karamoja and Turkana districts there were reports of incursions of large armed groups from Abyssinia interested in trade and ivory hunting, and possibly with an eye on territorial gains.

Instructions to the Commission

Considerable thought had been given to the question of an adjustment to the Sudan–Uganda boundary in the months before the Commission began its work. The first detailed proposals were made by Sir Reginald Wingate (Governor General of Sudan) to Viscount Kitchener in October 1911. Broadly speaking this involved transfer of the Lado enclave to Uganda and large tracts of northern Uganda south of latitude 5° N to Sudan. Several reasons were given, including the desirability of reuniting the Bari tribe which was divided by the existing border between Sudan and Uganda, and leaving the Turkana tribe exclusively within Uganda. Indeed, from the beginning it was made clear that the boundary 'should be a tribal one,' (FO 407/177 f. 43541, 27 October 1911). It was also noted that the territories to be transferred would be more accessible from their respective new administrative headquarters in Sudan and Uganda. A further objective was to place both banks of the Nile under a single administration to facilitate measures to combat sleeping sickness (FO 407/177 f. 4351, 21 October 1911). The Governor of Uganda, F. J. Jackson finally gave his response in March 1912 in which he argued for the inclusion of the Madi and Latuka tribes within Uganda east of the Nile, and the Kuku tribe within Uganda west of the Nile. This would have had the effect of placing the boundary along the Sanga river west of the Nile and along the Uma and upper Gomorro rivers east of the Nile. Significantly it would also have left Nimule and a navigable stretch of the Nile in Ugandan hands (Figure 2) (FO 407/177 f. 16972, 14 March 1912). Apart from the advantages of the boundary adjustment already noted by Wingate, the Governor of Uganda also believed that Sudan's occupation of part of the shore of Lake Rudolph would help prevent the smuggling of large quantities of rifles from Abyssinia. Wingate's response to Jackson's proposal was unequivocal; unless Sudan had access to the navigable stretch of the Nile from Nimule to Lake Albert (which meant possession of

Introduction

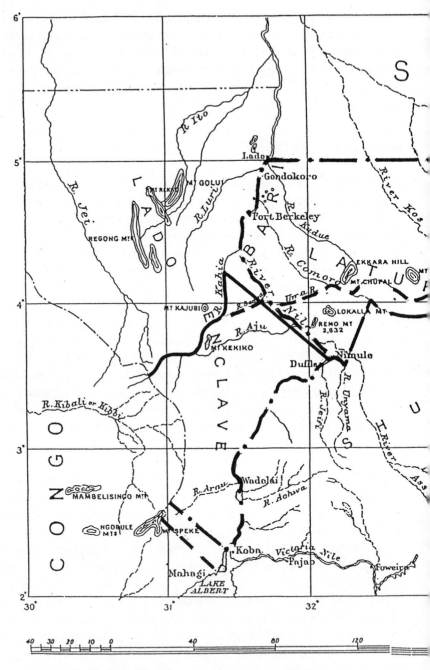

Figure 2. Sketch Plan showing suggested alteration in Uganda–Sudan Boundary (F.C. MacDonald, 27.2.12, F.O. 371/1361)

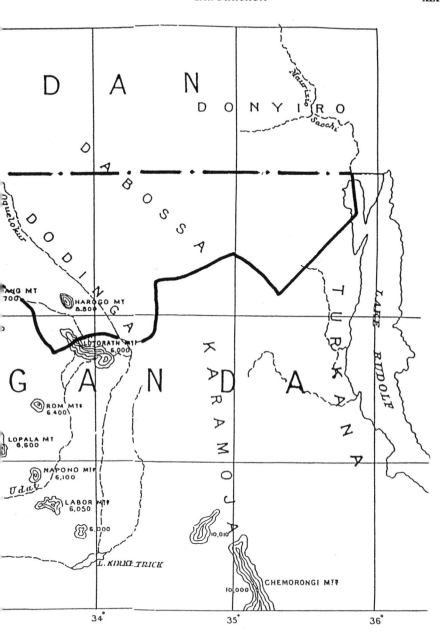

Existing boundary between Uganda and Sudan
Boundary proposed by Sudan
  „   „   „ Uganda

Nimule), the territorial transfer would not proceed (FO 407/177 F. 25592, 5 June 1912). The Colonial Office rapidly agreed that the Sudan government's proposals were acceptable, and the basis for the boundary delimitation between the Nile and Lake Rudolph remained as described by Wingate in October 1911 and repeated in his letter to Kitchener dated 5th November 1912:

> That the Soudan Government should take over that portion of the Uganda protectorate lying between the present boundary (5° north latitude) and a line commencing at the junction of the River Unyama with the Nile south of Nimule, thence proceeding up the River Unyama to a point on the right bank 10 miles from its mouth, from that point running in a north-north-easterly direction until it cuts 4° north latitude, thence roughly following 4° latitude taking in the Dodinga and Dabosa country, and finally turning up north-east to a point on the Sanderson Gulf on Lake Rudolf approximately where the shore of the gulf is cut by 4° 40′ north latitude. (FO 407/177 f. 48758)

In the latter months of 1912 arrangements were made for a boundary commission to convene to work out a detailed boundary delimitation. As late as November 1912 the Sudan government's representative was to be Major A. W. Jennings Bramly (20th Hussars). It is not clear when or why Major Jennings Bramly was replaced by Captain Kelly, but no more is heard about the Major in Foreign Office files. The Boundary Commission was not furnished with a very detailed brief, but Kelly and his associates would have known of the map prepared by the Foreign Office in February 1912 (Figure 2) and they no doubt had copies of Wingate's description of the proposed line quoted above. It is worth noting that Wingate's proposals eastwards of the Dodinga and Dabosa country were very vague. The official 1912 sketch map (Figure 2) shows a boundary which apears to take account of tribal lands in its eastern sector, although it is doubtful whether it was based on reliable information.

The work of the Commission

As officer in charge of the Boundary Commission Kelly had two chief functions to perform. First, the Commission had broad instructions from London as to the approximate alignment of the new Sudan–Uganda boundary, which would run from the White Nile in the vicinity of Nimule eastwards to the northern end of Lake Rudolph. The Commission was to devise a line which would not divide any single tribe between Sudan and Uganda, so that its greatest challenge was to identify suitable tribal boundaries. This was to prove extremely difficult, particularly in some of the densely populated highland regions. Secondly, Kelly himself was responsible for producing a basic survey map of the agreed boundary. To do this he was equipped with the basic instruments of the day, theodolites and compasses, with which he could record the bearings of prominent features, and calculate degrees of latitude with some accuracy. Kelly was often up early in the morning to take observations, even on days when there was a long march ahead. Early on in the trip he concluded that it was probably the wrong season for surveying because the view of distant hills was frequently obscured by mist, haze, and the smoke from bush fires. Nevertheless, he persisted with his survey work and achieved good results. To assist in this he had some maps provided by Pearson who was the chief surveyor of the Sudan Survey. These had no doubt been compiled using reports of travellers, army patrols, and officials but they were not very accurate. Kelly frequently found them to be unreliable, or that place-names were incorrect. To measure distance, Kelly made use of a perambulator wheel fitted with a mileometer, pushed along by his faithful servant Adam, who did not much enjoy the task. The noose around his neck (Plate 14) is presumably a joke, indicating that without such inducement he might have abandoned his pram-wheeling chore. In practice distances were recorded regularly until January 26th, but then more spasmodically according to the nature of the terrain. Sometimes, for speed, Kelly kept a rough note of distance, based on the speed of the camel.

Members of the Commission convened in Nimule on January 15th 1913 and on the same day a preliminary boundary arrangement was proposed, to be verified en route. The whole party then marched eastwards towards Madial which was reached in 32 days. On this stretch of the boundary the Commission functioned normally. The Uganda Commissioner Captain Tufnell was involved in discussions. There was considerable preoccupation with tribal limits, not least because it was the most populous region traversed by the boundary, and both Commissioners seemed keen to satisfy their respective governments. But all was not well. Kelly and Tufnell had very different ideas about the importance of trying to identify the tribal boundaries accurately. Tufnell was eager to finish the job and go on leave. One can hardly blame him; Tufnell had been in Africa for two years without leave, most of the time trying to control difficult tribes in northern Uganda.

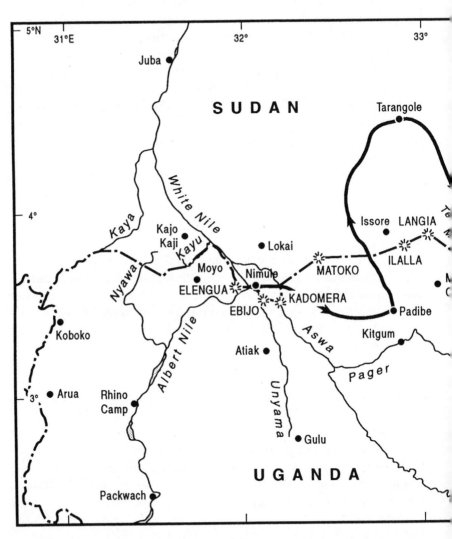

Figure 3. The Sudan–Uganda boundary today with an approximation of Kelly's journeys in 1913.

Not unreasonably, he believed he had a good knowledge of the tribes in the region. Rather surprisingly therefore Kelly and Tufnell sat down together in Madial on 17th February and drafted their recommendation on the boundary. They had covered approximately 120 miles of a boundary over 400 miles long. Although Kelly subsequently travelled further east as far as Jebel Mogila, which he reached on 28th February, the provisional boundary agreed with Tufnell was never modified. Thus only about 30 per cent of the Sudan–Uganda boundary was visited by the Commissioners, approximately 25 per cent was seen by Kelly alone, and the rest was never visited. On the face of it this was a most extraordinary performance by a Boundary Commission, and its work has been severely criticised by some writers and commentators (Collins 1962). It needs to be said however that to the west of the Nile, the Commissioners made it clear that their boundary recommendations 'will require verification and adjustment on the spot' (See Appendix 1 and 2). Similarly they recognised that the boundary from Jebel Mogila to Lake Rudolph, which Kelly could not visit because of lack of fodder and water, must 'remain for further consideration when the limits of the Turkana and Dabosa grazing grounds are more accurately known' (Appendix 1). As to the sector between Madial, where Tufnell left the Commission, and Jebel Mogila, Kelly was satisfied that their proposed line ran through sparsely inhabited territory, and did not divide any tribes. Subsequent experience appears to confirm that he was largely correct.

From the viewpoint of international boundary studies perhaps the most important feature of the diary is the effort made by Kelly and his colleagues in the first month of the Commission to find a boundary which would not divide the tribes. The difficulties in achieving this were very great, not least because of the complexity of African tribal relationships which neither Kelly nor Tufnell were qualified to understand in any depth. The evidence of local people was sometimes baffling and confusing, as Kelly notes on February lst, '... the information which I gained from them regarding the various hill people make the question of frontiers more complex than ever.' The guiding principle that tribes should not be divided was set aside when the interests of the colonial administration seemed more important. Thus the Commissioners delimited a small enclave to the south of Nimule to allow an adequate supply of labour to be available for Nimule which they knew would divide the Madi tribe. The justification for this was that in any case 'no unity exists among the various sections of the Madi tribe' (Appendix 1). Elsewhere mistakes were made which resulted in the division of some tribes, especially the northern Acholi who were divided from the greater part of their kinspeople in Uganda. However, the Commissioners admitted in their report that this could happen and recommended that 'small alterations' to the boundary could be made if this seemed necessary once the boundary was 'closely administered' (Appendix 2). Such an amendment was made in 1926 to reunite the 'Lango' people, by transferring part of Jebel Tereteinia to Uganda. As an alternative to subsequent adjustment of the boundary, the Commissioners were not averse to suggesting that the transplanting of a few villages may be desirable to achieve a thoroughly satisfactory boundary (Appendix 2).

To the west of the White Nile the Commissioners recommended a boundary which would leave the 'riverine people' below Nimule in the hands of Sudan. While noting that they had no first-hand experience of the region, they suggested an alignment to the Congo watershed involving use of the Khor Kayu, the Khor Nyaura, and finally the river Kaia. The official description of this sector includes the words ' .. to the thalweg of the Khor Kayu (Aju) upwards to its intersection with the thalweg of Khor Nyaura (Kigura) . . . ' (Brownlie 1979). In reality the Kayu and Nyaura are not connected. They are separate rivers. How was such an error introduced into the boundary description? A clue can perhaps be found in Kelly's diary of 18th February. He records that on the previous day he had a short talk with a man who said that 'a suitable boundary would be to follow up the Kayu river and then its tributary the Nyaura to its source . . . '. This inaccurate geographical information was recycled for several years. Elsewhere the Boundary Commission produced rather clearer descriptions of the boundary, making good use of prominent physical features and stretches of straight line.

In spite of its somewhat unusual approach to boundary delimitation, the 1913 Sudan–Uganda Boundary Commission recommended an alignment which survived largely unchallenged by either party. Some mistakes were made regarding tribal boundaries which have been partially rectified. There is continuing ambiguity over a short stretch of the boundary west of the White Nile which is supposed to follow 'the southern boundary of The Kuku tribe' which was never defined. More serious is the confusion over the Ilemi triangle and the grazing lands of the Turkana, currently administered by Kenya. Kelly had made it clear that this ought to be resolved before the boundary was agreed, but his advice was not heeded. Overall, he seems to have been satisfied with the results of his work, particularly from a Sudanese viewpoint. Control of the Nile as far as Nimule was secured for Sudan, together with access to the waters of Lake Rudolph (Turkana) around Sanderson Bay (Figure 3), as required in the instructions to the Commission.

Subsequent history of the boundary

Kelly penned his final report on the Sudan–Uganda Boundary Commission to the Governor General of Sudan from his camp on the river Lotilleit on 22nd April 1913. At the time Kelly was still on his way to the Boma plateau. His excursion towards the Abyssinian boundary was shortlived because of his encounter with large groups of armed and hostile Abyssinians (Plate 18). By 12th June Kelly had returned to the safety of Pibor post in Sudan (Plate 19) where he wrote long reports to the Governor General about the political situation to the east.

The Sudan–Uganda boundary was formally declared by Order of the Secretary of State dated 21st April 1914, following the recommendations of the Commission very closely. For reasons which are not clear, Kelly's Commission names physical features of the boundary from west to east, while the Order in Council chooses to give them from east to west. On 17th September 1926 by Order of the Secretary of State a relatively small area of the Tereteinia foothills was transferred from Sudan to Uganda in the interests of tribal unity. Another reason given for the transfer was that it would facilitate sleeping sickness control (Collins 1962). In the same year the Rudolph Province of Uganda was transferred to Kenya. This meant the loss of a large area of territory north of the Turkwell river (Figure 3), while approximately 140 miles of the former boundary recommended in 1913 became the Sudan–Uganda border. This sector has not been without its problems, which remain unresolved to this day. Kelly's Commission warned that the proposed line east from Jebel Harogo to Lake Rudolph would require further consideration when Turkana and Dabosa grazing grounds were better known. The 1914 Order in Council described the line as running from Jebel Mogila (which is to the north of Jebel Harogo) east to Lake Rudolph 'following a straight line or such a line as would leave to Uganda the customary grazing grounds of the Turkana tribe' (Brownlie 1979). When these grazing grounds were identified by the mutual agreement of Sudanese and Ugandan officials in 1931 they extended considerably north of the proposed line. The limits of the grazing grounds were outlined by a Red Line which involves a northerly extension of Kenyan administration especially in an area known as the Ilemi triangle (Figure 3). There is disagreement between the parties as to whether the Red Line boundary is provisional, or whether it forms the basis for an international boundary. Alternatives have been proposed but never agreed, and the potential for serious disagreement remains.

The Sudan–Uganda international boundary is some 270 miles (435 km) long, and the Sudan–Kenya international boundary is some 140 miles (225 km) long.

Glossary

(Ar. = Arabic)
(coll. Ar. = colloquial Arabic)

Abied	(Ar. *'abid*, slaves) Derogatory term used by northern Sudanese to signify southern Sudanese
Amerikani	Type of imported (literally American) cloth, popular in tribal markets
Ardeb	(Ar. *irdabb*) Measure of volume = 198 litres
Arderib	Probably *ardeib* (coll. Ar.), tamarind (*Tamarindus indica*), a large hardwood tree
Askari	East African British-trained native soldier
Bandanna	Coloured handkerchief usually with yellow or white spots
Bandar	(or banda) a hut
Belk	Meaning unclear. Possibly another kind of gum?
Bimbashi	(coll. Ar. from Turkish) Major
Burma	(Ar.) Large earthenware containers for transporting grain or water
Chignon	Coil of hair worn at the back of the head
Deleib palm	*Deleib* (coll. Ar.) (*Borassus aethiopum*), a large fan palm with a large variety of practical uses.
Dhurra	(coll. Ar.) Sorghum or giant millet (*Sorghum vulgare*)
Dijdij	Dik dik — a very small antelope about 18″ high
Dukhn	(coll. Ar. *dukhun*) Food grain bullrush millet (*Pennisetum typhoidum*), grown chiefly in sandy regions
Fellakeb	*Falakab* (coll. Ar.), a kind of stick used for thatching houses
Ful Sudani	(coll. Ar.) Groundnuts (*Arachis hypogaea*)
Fula	(coll. Ar.) Large excavated pool
Gail'd	To take a siesta; Ar. *gayyala*
Garrah	A gourd; Ar. *qar'a*
Gemeiza tree	(Ar. *jummayza*) A very large wild fig tree (*Ficus sycomorus*)
Ghaba	Forest (Ar.)
Ginga	Village grain store
Girba	(Ar. *girba*) Large leather water-skin
Gugins	Village grain store
Hagliq	*Heglig* (coll. Ar.) A large tree of limited economic value (*Balanites aegyptiaca*)
Haifir	(coll. Ar. *hafir*) Large pit excavated in clay to act as a reservoir, filling up in the rainy season. Identical with fula (above)
Hamla	(Ar.) Train of pack animals or baggage train on the march

Hashab	(coll. Ar.) A shrubby tree yielding good quality commercial gum (*Acacia senegal*)
Helio	Message signalled by using a heliograph, which reflects flashes of sunlight by means of moving mirrors
Jackson	A Jackson gazelle
Jebel	(Ar.) Hill, mountain, rocky outcrop
Jolly	Slang for excursion or trip, possibly from Ar. *jawla*, a patrol or tour
Kaimakam	(Ar./Turkish) Lieutenant Colonel
Katib	(Ar.) Clerk
Khor	(coll Ar.) Dry valley
Kurbag	(coll. Ar *Kurbaj*) whip of rhinoceros hide
Kokab	(coll. Ar.) Spear
Kujur	(coll. Ar. *Kujur*) Witch doctor
Lu-luing	High-pitched noise made by tribal women at times of anger, excitement, or celebration, achieved by rapid vibration of the tongue
Mablak tree	Unidentified
Malod	Short-handled tool for land preparation
Mamur	(Ar.) A district officer
Matama	Local term for red *dhurra*
Mek	(coll. Ar.) Shilluk tribal chief
Mul. Tan.	*Mulazim tani* (coll. Ar.) Second Lieutenant
Neghil grass	*Nagil* (coll. Ar.), *Cynodon dactylon*
Nyau	A small red opaque bead
Onbashi	(coll. Ar. from Turkish) Corporal in Sudanese regiment
Palaver	Prolonged discussion or debate between tribespeople
Piastre	Coin; one-hundredth of an Egyptian pound
Piga	To hit (used of raiding)
Ravar	Meaning unclear
Rotl	(coll. Ar.) Unit of weight (0.99 lbs or 449.28 grammes)
Rowyan	A type of bead (colour not known)
Rupee	Indian currency common in East Africa
Salaam	(Ar.) Muslim greeting; literally 'peace (be on you)'
Sayal	(coll. Ar.) Moderate-sized acacia (*Acacia Sieberiana*)
Sesame (sim-sim)	Valuable plant used for oil and food (*Sesamum orientale*)
Shawish	(coll. Ar. from Turkish) Sergeant
Shens	A branch of the Shilluk tribe
Shenzi	The implication is of an inferior person
Sirdar	(coll. Ar. from Turkish) Commander-in-chief of the Egyptian army; at this time the office was held by the Governor-General of the Sudan, i.e. Wingate
Subagh	A large tree, probably *subakh* (coll. Ar.), (*Terminalia brownei*)
Syce	(coll. Ar.) Horse groom
Tarbush	(coll. Ar.) Rimless cap, similar to the fez, commonly worn by Muslims in North Africa

Tartib	(Ar.) Daily routine or programme
Telabun	(coll. Ar.) Finger millet (*Eleusine coracana*), one of the main grain crops of Equatoria
Temerghi	(coll. Ar. *tamarji*) Sudanese medical orderly
Tiang	The Korrigum (*Damaliscus Korrigum*)
Tombak	(coll. Ar. *tumbak*) Tobacco
Tse tse fly	Biting fly found commonly in central Africa which carries the trypanasome causing sleeping sickness, often fatal to people and animals
Wakil	(Ar.) Agent
Wimbi	Local term for telbun
Yuzbashi	(coll. Ar. from Turkish); Captain
Zeilan	A blue bead (said to be the favourite among tribespeople)
Zeriba	(Ar.) Compound enclosed by thorn fence to protect animals. 'Zeriba'd' villages were stockaded settlements. The term is also used of the square formation adopted by a force on the march.

Abbreviations

ADC	Assistant District Commissioner
DC	District Commissioner
BEA	British East Africa
C in C	Commander-in-Chief
KAR	King's African Rifles
MO	Medical Officer
NCO	Non-Commissioned Officer
OC	Officer Commanding
RH	Rest House
SS	Steam Ship

THE DIARY

1

Assembly and Preparations

December 10th 1912–January 18th 1913

Kelly, accompanied by four British officers, makes the 33–day journey by steamer to their first camp on the bank of the Nile opposite Rejaf. Another steamer brings camels, donkeys, and mules, together with other equipment and supplies. There is to be a large escort, to which the Sudanese contribute 30 infantry, 100 camel corps with their officers, plus a field hospital and veterinary support. They proceed by land to Nimule, over 90 miles away, with Kelly and a small party going ahead, arriving after an eight-day march. For part of the route they are accompanied by a Ugandan official, ADC Weatherhead.

At Nimule they are joined by Captain Tufnell, the Uganda representative on the Commission, and half a company (50 men?) of the KAR commanded by Captain Lilley. There are discussions about the boundary with Anderson (Acting Province Commissioner from Buttinba), Postlethwaite (ADC of the Acholi District) and More (ADC of Nimule). Kelly is already concerned that insufficient grain, and grain of the wrong kind, has been collected by the Uganda contingent. He is also disturbed that Tufnell would like to use the escort for punitive action against the Dodinga hillmen, which could prejudice the work of the commission.

Dec. 10th 1912   Left Khartoum in SS Tamai 12 noon.
Dove and Bruce on board.

Dec. 11th   Dueim 6.30 pm.

Dec. 12th   Wood station 4.30 am to 9.00 am. Kosti 3 pm.

Dec. 13th   Wooding at Renk wood station 1 pm. Passed Renk 3.30 pm.

Dec. 14th   Passed Melut 9 pm.

Dec. 15th   Kodok 4.30 am–10 am. Taufikia 10 pm–midnight. Saw Logan and gave him letter for C. H. Walker re his going to Magi. He also had wire from Clayton on same subject which indicated that he should go there while I was at Boma — which I do not want.

Dec. 16th   Wooded[1] during night at Khor Attar. Tonga 11–12.20 visited new bridge.

Dec. 17th   In Sudd.[2]

Dec. 18th   Sudd. Hillat el Nuer 12 noon–1 pm.

Dec. 19th   Sudd. Passed Shambe about midnight.

Dec. 20th   Kenisa wood station 12.30 pm.

Dec. 21st   Bor 3–4 pm.

Dec. 22nd   Sheikh Tombe midnight. Gigging 8 am. Tried channel above Gigging but found it impassable, so had to return below Tombe and other channel.

Dec. 23rd   Arrived Mongalla 9 am. Owen wired to Commandant Ferris. Bruce to send Beir policeman Omar Derwish in, if available.

Dec. 23rd–2nd Jan.   At Mongalla. Messed with Harman[3] and Powell.[4] Christmas dinner with Owen.[5] Darley[6] had waited since Dec. 2nd for

---

[1] Nile river steamers were fuelled by wood, necessitating frequent replenishment and supplies.

[2] The Sudd is an extensive area of swamp through which the upper Nile waters flow. It constitutes a major impediment to communications.

[3] F. de W. Harman (Norfolk Regiment) was a Major (Bimbashi) in the 12th Sudanese Regiment. Placed in command of the Commission's escort, Kelly regarded him as efficient, energetic and competent.

[4] J. Powell (Royal Army Medical Corps) was a Lieutenant-Colonel (Kaimakam) in the Egyptian army, seconded to the Commission as a Medical Officer. He specialised in treatment of sleeping sickness.

[5] RCR Owen, Governor of Mongalla Province and later a Provincial Governor in southern Egypt. He served on the Sinai boundary commission in 1906. See Plate 4. Another Owen features as a Medical Officer of the Northern Patrol (13 February, 14 March).

[6] Henry Darley, a British ex-army officer well known as a trader, ivory hunter and adventurer. He knew the region extremely well and appears to have been sought for information and advice.

me and received £E1 per diem till Jan. 2nd and food for his porters. Could not arrange any definite arrangement with him as he was very uncertain as to his future plans and movements. Owen wrote him a letter embodying my requirements. I finally arranged verbally that if he does go to Boma and cares to await my arrival, I may take him on at £E1 a day.

He spoke of sending down to the Kuroni river to meet me and in parting said he might go to Lolimi.

2nd Jan. 1913 S.S. Nazir arrived 1 pm, Hannek at 7 pm, Huddleston[7] in charge on latter.

3rd Jan. Both steamers left at 9.45 am. The company of the 12th Sudanese under Harman were played down to the landing place by Owen's police band. The combination of Auld Lang Syne vilely played and the old ladies of the harimat lu-luing and dancing headed by the Sheikha armed with a spear was really comic.

Tied up for night below Gondokoro channel.

Jan. 4th Arrived at entrance of channel at 6 am. I went up in rowing boat with Huddleston to see Weatherhead, Asst. District Commissioner of Gondokoro. Found Bruce[8] with him — he had left Rejaf on the 26th, gone to Kajo-Kaji and returned to Rejaf on the 31st (80 miles each way). Yesterday had gone down in a dug out to Mongalla, found we had left and marched back arriving at Gondokoro at midnight. Arranged with Weatherhead[9] to write to Nimule for grain and flour — I thought Owen had arranged this before and it is now rather a nuisance that we shall have to carry our full ten days reserve forage from Rejaf as we shall not know if Nimule can supply or not. Bruce came on with us. Weatherhead asked for return of all rifles and ammunition[10] and said it was necessary to take out licences at once if we want to shoot

---

[7] H. J. Huddleston (Dorset Regiment) was a Major in the Egyptian army and Sudanese Camel Corps. He commanded the Camel Corps men in the escort, and was responsible for transport. Governor-General of the Sudan 1940–47. Died in 1950.

[8] The Honourable R. Bruce, Major in the Egyptian army. Acted as supplies and intelligence Officer. Kelly regarded him as resourceful and indefatigable.

[9] Weatherhead was Assistant District Commissioner of Gondokoro in Uganda. He accompanied the Commission from 7th to 11th January when the boundary of his district was reached.

[10] 'Return' = record of. There was great sensitivity about illegal ivory poaching at the time, which may explain Weatherhead's rather bureaucratic demand.

elephants on the way. £20 to shoot one, £40 for two, the second £20 is returned if only one or no elephant is shot.

Went on 9.30 am. A civilian driver fell overboard from the Nazir and was not seen again; Harman who was on board said the man was standing on the connecting cable between steamer and barge. There was no boat on the Hannek and by the time we had lowered ours, 10 minutes was lost.

Arrived at cleared landing place opposite Rejaf at 6 pm. Got all animals on shore and cleared two barges by 9 pm.

Jan. 5th   Moved into camp. Nazir left us at 6.15 to bring up two barges which had to be left near Lado owing to difficulties of navigation. Arrived at 4 pm, discharged by 5.30 pm. Hannek was finished with at 11.30 am and left for north at 1 pm. I went over to Rejaf in afternoon to see Castle-Smith.

Jan. 6th   Nazir left for north at daylight. Tamai with Owen on board and Amara, post boat, arrived during morning. Former left in afternoon for mouth of Kir river where Owen is to disembark.

Jan. 7th   Amara picked up mails and left for north at 6 am. Tamai returned, took surplus rations etc. over to Rejaf north and took other stores not required to Mongalla, Dempster in charge. Mul. Tan. Mustafa Eff. Fahmi reported for going to Rejaf without permission.

Having published orders on the 5th, putting Harman in command of escort, Huddleston in charge of all transport and Mersal Eff. Abd El Latif 12th Sudanese in charge of donkeys, Bruce in charge of supplies — I handed over the charge of the whole push to Harman for good. Asked him to practice during march to Nimule making camp in square at night, getting into square from column of route on march etc, so that we shall be ready for all eventualities on road. Powell and I left camp at 2.30 pm leaving escort to leave on the 9th midday; the donkeys especially require time to stretch their legs and recover from the journey, they were very closely packed on board and being mostly small and weak, they are certainly not able for hard work at once. The camels are reported by Huddleston to be fair, though a proportion are too light for hamla work. Having to carry 10 days reserve forage, the animals will be very heavily loaded at first, even though the men will carry 3 days rations on them and camel corps are going dismounted.

Actual strength is Harman (Norfolk Regt.) in command of escort and of company 12th Sudanese, Huddleston (Dorset Regt.) in charge of transport and section of Camel Corps, Bruce (Argyll and Suth. Highdrs.) Intelligence Officer and in charge of supplies. Powell (RAMC) who was originally sent up for Sleeping Sickness work and who at his own request and mine is coming to Rudolf.

Company 12th Sudanese 100 strong, 3 native officers
Section Camel Corps (Sudanese), 30 strong, 1 native officer
½ Section Field Hospital with Syrian doctor Haddad Eff.
Veterinary temerghis with Egyptian officer Salib Eff.
Native transport officer
50 camels, 320 donkeys, 20 mules.

Powell and I found Owen and Weatherhead at Nyonki (Sh. Tchobi), rest house, good cleared road 15' wide, 9 miles along road.

Jan. 8th Marched to Shindirru (Sh. Lejju) 12 miles. Took latitude and azimuths to all hills in sight. Unluckily impossible to see any distant points owing to haze from grass fires etc. This is evidently not the season for surveying.

Jan. 9th Marched to Kirrillu 10¾ mls. Took latitude and azimuths on all hills.

Jan. 10th Marched to Fagar R. H. (Sh. Lenchu) 8½ miles. Powell and I left camp at 3.15 pm and reached top of Jebel Kunangi in an hour with carriers. Fine view from top (800' above plain) spoilt by haze. Fixed reference point in evening but too much haze to take round of angles. Latitude after dinner. Very strong wind during night but not cold.

Jan. 11th Most unluckily impossible to see any distant points, I had hoped to pick up Belinian and Gumbiri from here, thus fixing place definitely. Took a round of angles on visible points and reached camp at 9.15 am. Breakfasted and marched to 1 pm, halted till 3 and reached camp at Uma river rest house at 4.30 pm, 12 miles. This is the end of the Bari district and Weatherhead comes no further with us. The country is of course dried up now but there is plenty of variety of scenery, in fact from the point of view of a hurried survey there is too much wealth of detail in the shape of hills and complicated hydrography. Most of the khors still have water in pools, the bush is mostly small and not thick. Apparently the whole country is much depopulated, probably the Baris never recovered from the forays of the slave traders in Baker's time.[11] They are a most peaceful lot now, very different from the truculent warriors he described then. Weatherhead maintains they are an overflow of various inland tribes — Nymbara, Fajollu, Latuka etc. and that they are a race of comparatively recent origin.

Their language is akin to the two former and has traces of Galla as has the Latuka talk. There is no cohesion amongst them and even the headmen have little authority over the remainder. I was struck by the strict control which the Ugandan officials have over them. I obtained a few details from Weatherhead regarding the existing administration as he goes no further with us than this, the boundary of his district.

Nobody except the riverain Baris are apparently administered at all although occasionally people come in from Lokoya, Lafit and Latuka to salaam or to bring complaints (which however are not dealt with unless they involve absolutely no difficulty). There is an uninhabited zone, 20 miles wide, between the Baris and the hill people, except for the few Baris who have established themselves at the foot of the Lokoya hills to escape taxation. The tax is levied per head — 7000 rupees being collected last year (from the Baris only) at 3 rupees per head of taxpayers.[12] A crown land rent of 2 rupees a plot — which amounts to a hut-tax — is levied in Gondokoro.

There are a few Baris at the foot of the Gumussi hills (chief Lorolokaiyimba of Ladei) and of Lomeji. In the Mongalla province on the other hand, a tax is levied on sheep and goats (2 rps on head of *cattle*) and there is a forced sale of dhurra at 30 P.T. the *ardeb*.

It is to be noted that in Uganda, the chiefs of villages are responsible for the cleanliness of roads on either side of them and for the upkeep of rest houses. The 'river road' is now closed — except by special permit — on account of 'fly'.

Jan. 12th The road now leaves the hill groups behind and enters a heavily undulating country, wooded and with bush and small trees mostly, the soil being sandy or gravel with occasional granite outcrops. The Uma river is now dry 110' wide with sandy bed, pools here and

[11] Sir Samuel Baker (1821–93) explored the upper reaches of the Nile with his wife between 1860 and 1864. Later (1869–73) he commanded an expedition on behalf of the Khedive of Egypt to suppress slavery and annex territory in the equatorial Nile region. For his account of the Bari, see his books, *The Albert N'yanza* and *Ismailia*.

[12] Rupees were common currency in Uganda and British East Africa at that time.

there: for the first time I noticed 'fly' — the ordinary animal *tse tse* — on this stretch of road. Camp at Kirrippi (nearer sheikh Vunni) at 15¾ miles — a very hot tiring march, especially so as we started only at 6.15 am — a bad 'tartib'. A few Madis came into camp, an intelligent man Voga brother of the sheikh amongst others — they have 3 incisors of the lower jaw extracted whereas the Acholi have two out. As elsewhere water in khor close to rest house.

Jan. 13th Another long march of 15 miles, the last six being entirely without shade and the only wooding being small subagh trees stunted by grass fires. The Rest House is only 300 yards from the Assua, a pretty river which still had running water about 250′ wide with 10′ banks. In the flood season, there is no possibility of crossing except by boat as the current is very strong.

For the first time during the march from Rejaf, Powell got something to shoot — a Jackson — there has been an extraordinary dearth of animal life, hardly a spoor even to be seen.

Jan. 14th A very hot march over mostly stony ground 10½ miles to Nimule Post which is about a mile from the Nile where the latter takes a sharp bend. Found More the Asst. District Commissioner and Lilley of the KAR (who takes half a company out as the Uganda Escort). Walked in the evening to the Unyama-Nile junction, the former river which was laid down theoretically as the beginning of the boundary is some 80′ wide and 5′ deep over near the junction, but shallows rapidly higher up at this season and is crossed knee deep, though in the rains it has a very strong current and is crossed by a ferry boat. Dined and lunched with More whose house is close to the Rest Huts where we camped.

Jan. 15th Anderson the acting Province Commissioner arrived from Buttiaba by steamer Baker yesterday evening with his wife, and came up to camp at 8 am. Tufnell[13] the Uganda representative on the Com-

---

[13] H. M. Tufnell (1872–1952). Commissioned into the KAR. Tufnell reached the rank of Captain before joining the Uganda Civil Service in 1908 as an ADC. By 1912 he was DC for Rudolf Province, which included responsibility for the Northern Garrison (formerly the Northern Patrol), charged with preventing raids and disarming tribes. Among those who resisted British rule most were the mountain tribes of the Agoro, Logire, Tereteinia and Didinga ranges which lay close to the boundary adjustment. This helps explain Tufnell's attitude to the people which was often at odds with Kelly's. (Barber, 1968, pp. 121–124).

mission and Postlethwaite, the ADC of the Acholi district, came in
from east during the morning.

Owen, Anderson, Tufnell and myself discussed the boundary with
the help of More and Postlethwaite for the Madi and Acholi tribal
boundaries which are both a source of difficulty. We arrived at a preliminary arrangement which we can verify en route; it apparently makes a
satisfactory dividing line through the Madi who must anyhow be split up.

I was rather upset to find that all the grain collected by Uganda
for us is 'telaban' locally called 'Wimbi' which is not at all good for
donkeys and which I doubt if camels will eat at all. More, whom I
asked through Weatherhead to collect 12000 lbs of dhurra here, apparently thought this requisition could be filled by the grain sent out to
Madial (12 days east, the Uganda post in Nyangiya) and made no
arrangement at all. The news about water and routes east of Madial is
also disconcerting; it is evident that the present is not the time of the
year which should have been chosen and the beginning of the rains
would have been far better both for grazing, water and incidentally for
survey purposes, for at present it is impossible to see any distance at
all and my map will be limited to a compass traverse. Tufnell says the
fly is deadly along the Kideppo river which makes the trip no more
easy. He was very anxious that we should take on the Dodinga hillmen
who have been raiding the Dodosi for some time and have taken over
4000 head of cattle from them in all. He was quite right in saying that
the situation would be difficult unless we take over and administer the
Dodinga at once, since Uganda will have their post within a day's
march of them. I made it clear that we can take no part in any punitive
measures anywhere and in talking to Anderson and Postlethwaite
afterwards dissuaded them from making any use of our march through
Agoro to drive off some truculent people from the top of the hill — I
explained that in any case the march of our large force would be
looked upon with distrust by the natives and that if we do anything at
all in the way of repression, the news will go ahead of us and by no
means pave the way as we would wish.

I was not a little surprised to hear the way the Uganda people
talked of their dealings with the natives; they certainly believe in
'*fortiter in modo*'[14] and appear to think nothing of taking cattle and
grain by force wherever they go.

We had our meals with the Andersons who are both nice people;

[14] 'Fortiter in modo' is probably a deliberate misquotation from Lord Chesterfield (1752)
'suauiter in modo, fortiter in re' — gentle in manner, resolute in action. In Kelly's view the
Uganda people acted toughly towards the natives.

she has been over two years up here at Masindi or on trek with her husband. She apparently goes everywhere with him, shoots and is altogether of the Lady Baker stamp, though young and nice looking. I wrote to Mrs Kennedy asking her to look her up in Khartoum when she goes through from Gondokoro by next mail.

I arranged with the representatives of Ali Dinar the big Indian merchant of Uganda to send out 10 rolls of iron[15] wire to Madial; Tufnell has promised to write to Clothier who is in command there to send out and try and buy dhurra at Morongole.

Jan. 16th I went in a dug out with Powell, More and Ferris the captain of the 'Baker' down the Unyama to the mouth and thence in an iron boat down the Nile to see the lie of the land. The steamers now tie up upstream of the Unyama mouth and goods are generally lightered up this river to Nimule. Ferris does not know the river between this point and the rapids which are about 1000 yards lower down but thinks there may be a suitable channel. There is no suitable place for a river side post where the steamer ties up nor in the southern peninsula at the junction, but just before the rapids there is firm ground to the river bank, a gentle rise for 150 yards, then a line of high ground 50–150' high where the old military post was when the Belgians occupied Dufile. If then a channel can be found, a wharf could be made here and the railway carried along the bottom of the hill either by the rivers route or inland, the post being built on the high ground.[16]

Jan. 17th I expected the escort in the morning but Weatherhead came in early and said they were staying at the Assua river as the donkeys were in need of rest. Bruce came in after lunch. Two camels had been shot on the way — the same two which were ill at Rejaf and two donkeys died. More sent out to try and change 'telabun' flour for 'matama' unground (red dhurra) but said he had plenty of telabun grain here if required.

Jan. 18th The escort arrived about 10 am and camped in a spot nearer the Unyama than our camp which had been cleared by More yesterday.

---

[15] Iron wire was much in demand for making arm and leg decorations, and for general use.
[16] The Sudanese government wished to acquire Nimule to facilitate river trade upstream. Kelly prepared a sketch of possible arrangements for a new port there. He regarded the facilities as poor (January 18th). A copy of his sketch is in the Sudan Archive at Durham (SAD 186/1/297).

The Andersons and Weatherhead went north to the Fula rapids (5 miles) in the afternoon; Tufnell, Postlethwaite and Lilley going out to Lokai. Anderson received a wire saying we could have free licences for shooting except elephant — this was in reply to his request. We had at Gondokoro had to take out £20 licences which included one elephant, and we are now due for a £10 refund but have to pay £20 to shoot a second elephant. Huddleston arrived about 5.30 pm having shot a small elephant and had an adventure with a rhino within a mile of Nimule which had charged without provocation. Nimule is by no means a place to linger in longer than necessary so I decided to move on tomorrow, resting at Lokai.

Moore proved a very broken reed about grain, only 800 lbs of 'matama' arriving and the unlimited quantity of telabun promised dwindling down to 1600 lbs, so that we are only carrying about 5 days ration from here. I made a deal with Ali Dinar the local merchant for him to buy two bales of 'Amerikani' cloth which we brought for trade goods; we got about the same price as it cost in Khartoum and bought iron wire instead.

The Government buildings at Nimule are hardly worth taking over at all, they are the ADC's house a long two roomed building in stone with a verandah all round (not a bad type of house and well built), the office (2 roomed), guard room, Post office, Hospital, Doctor's and Clerk's houses. The doctor and clerk are both Indians.

I had a short talk yesterday with the Mamur of Kadjo-Kadji our post in the Kuku country who had just been touring the Lugware district. He said a suitable boundary between the latter and the Kuku would be to follow up the Kayu river and then its tributary the Nyaura to its source, then to the Kaia which would be followed up to the Congo watershed. There seems no doubt that in getting the Lugware, the Uganda Government are getting more than an exchange for what they are giving us; it is a fertile country with an industrious population and an excellent climate.

2

Excursion to the Farajok District

January 19th–February 13th

The Commission and its escort set out for Madial, but after five days it is decided to split into three groups to make a more thorough survey of the tribes in the boundary area and to the north. Kelly goes north to Farajok, Obbo and Tarangole with Huddleston and 20 camel corps. Tufnell dislikes the delay this will cause in proceeding along the boundary to the east. The parties meet up again in Madial. Kelly notes difficulties in preparing a basic survey of the route because haze and smoke from bush fires prevent observations, and every hill seems to be given several names by the local tribes.

Jan. 19th   After some delay in getting the grain from Moore, the last of the column got out of camp about 6.15 am. The camels caused fresh astonishment amongst the people who otherwise seemed to take our appearance calmly.

A sandy march by a cleared 12′ track mostly through open slightly undulating country to Lokai, a rest post ½ mile from the Assua river near the Madi village of Alimmu, 10 miles from Nimule, where we found the Uganda contingent in camp. In the afternoon I had a talk with Tufnell, Moore and Postlethwaite regarding the Madi boundary which is a little difficult to arrange as any boundary that is taken must divide this tribe between the two Governments. Tufnell and I agreed that we would in our report suggest that the Uma river should form the boundary between us as this is the natural Bari-Madi boundary. In order to provide for an eventual railway, it would seem simple to insert a clause providing for a right of way. We decided however on a line which coincides more or less with the theoretical one laid down already.

We managed to get about 1200 lbs of matama and telabun mixed here which will slightly improve the situation and I got Postlethwaite to send a runner to his post at Kitgum in the Acholi country to try and divert the 100 Bunyoro porters — who are bringing grain from Unyoro to Madial — on to the main road from here to the latter so that if necessary we can draw on what they carry on our way out. I had agreed with Anderson that he should engage an additional 100 porters (besides those just mentioned) in order to expedite the transport to Madial where he now promises 6 tons of grain on the 2nd February. This was necessary as our first request only asked for the grain to be delivered in the middle of March at their eastern most post. All this supply of grain was omitted from my estimates approved by Bernard as I expected to buy locally with trade goods. Unless our animals last out much better than seems now likely, I am afraid the estimates will be much exceeded.

Jan. 20th   We rested the day at Lokai to give the animals a chance. I spent the day working out my observations and plotting my map which so far is quite satisfactory in spite of being able to get no long theodolite shots. Finally settled with Tufnell the Madi frontier line which gives us enough Madi to supply labour for the Nimule post and still leaves it possible to administer from Kadjo-Kadji. In the afternoon I walked to the tin hut 1000 yards from the camp which was erected by the Uganda people at the time when it was intended to move the District Commissioner's headquarters here from Nimule for reasons of health. However it was afterwards decided to have the headquarters at Gulu which is about 70 miles south and 30 miles from the river and it was then necessary to keep an ADC at Nimule and wash out Lokai. I see no advantages about the latter; though it is higher and less shut in than Nimule, it is by no means a health resort in the rains.

   I afterwards walked down to the Assua river with Moore and by it to camp. It is a pretty river and must be a ***** fine body of water in the rains. At present it has only about 20′ × 1′ of running water in its sandy bed which is over 200′ wide. The parties sent out to shoot meat were not very successful and a bush buck was the only result. It is most unlucky that game is so scarce, as the reduced biscuit ration issued to the men is hardly enough to keep them going.

Jan. 21st   The Uganda escort with their carriers cleared camp in front of our advanced guard which got off about 5.45 am. An uninteresting march over burnt undulating country with scanty small trees. Crossed the Assua ¾ mile from camp without difficulty as the banks had been ramped by a working party yesterday. I marched in rear to sketch and got into camp about 10.15 am, 10 miles, at rest huts Padwat.

   Here we are in the Acholi country and the chief Munusala and some of his men had turned out in full kit — leopard skins thrown over their shoulders, oblong shields 4½ feet long with horn corners and a black pompom on the lower ends, spears, ostrich feathers in their hair which is matted in the Shilluk style but mostly cut off. Some of them wore the very unwholesome looking circular wrist knives which I believe they use with great effect at close quarters. Slung close round the neck is a goat's horn covered with leather and wrapped ***** with ***** narrow flat iron wire, the top covered with a cap which is [used for a signal]. I got the chief in and with Tufnell through Postlethwaite's interpreter gave him a talk to explain why we had come.

We will see, I hope, a good number of these people at Agwak so it is no use writing about them now.

The boundary agreed upon runs about 10 miles north of and parallel to this road (cleared to 15') on which we are marching; this runs through an uninhabited country (except for a few Acholi who can be moved) and leaves all the Acholi except some mixed people of the Farajok district to Uganda. It is difficult to make the boundary here as the Acholi, Madi and Latuka all mix near their tribal limits which are thus almost impossible to define.

Water had to be dug for in Kh. Nyimwuri at this camp Padwat; Bruce goes on ahead of the advanced guard arranges camp and has the use of the tools carried by the advanced guard to clear any obstacles, dig for water etc. The 'tartib' of the march and camp works very well indeed thanks to Harman, Huddleston and Bruce. Tufnell has most alarming ideas about the Boma plateau trip and its difficulties, but we may hear more about it at Madial. In the afternoon I went to a small hill Atero near camp but there was as usual too much haze to do any good.

Jan. 22nd The escort and hamla got off before daylight and I followed as usual as I have to wait for light for sketching. A slight delay in crossing Khor Nyimwur where Bruce made a ramp up the banks with the advance guard. I find the names of hills most puzzling and almost impossible to find with any hope of accuracy; I have had as many as four different names for the same hill from people at different villages. The whole work of mapmaking is very trying now owing to the absolute impossibility of seeing any distant points.

The day's march was 13¾ miles to the rest huts of Palabek where the Acholi chief had cleared a large space, brought up water etc. The people here are nearly all dressed in tarbushes and suits of clothes; it seems a great pity when they have such an extraordinarily picturesque dress themselves that they should take to wearing shabby European clothes. I tried to buy some curios, shields etc, but found the people have very large ideas about their money value, possibly because they do not know the value of money — I was asked 25 rupees for a shield and 5 rupees for a small head ornament. We hear that at tomorrow's camp there was a fight with the neighbouring village in which three men were killed on each side; the quarrel began over the meat of a hartebeest which had been killed. Postlethwaite the ADC of this district is anxious to settle the question of fines while the troops are here but I am most unwilling to allow this as I do not want reports to go ahead of our bellicose tendencies. I am beginning to think we shall do little good by marching straight through to Madial as Tufnell wishes, it seems to me that if we do, we might as well have settled the boundary entirely in the office at Nimule. I think it important to find out something of the Farajok district, north of this, which falls to us and of the north part of the Agoro hills of which the Ugandan people know nothing but which they believe to be inhabited by a mixture of Acholi and Latuka. Tufnell is not at all keen in delaying as he has no money to feed his men after the beginning of March and moreover is anxious to go on leave. I think now we are here, it would be quite wrong to make no effort to find out all we can about the debateable country. To go round the north end of Agoro will delay us about ten days but I think we can leave the infantry and hamla at the south end where there is plenty of food to go round the north with the Camel Corps section. However we can decide better when we reach the hill.

Jan. 23rd   A march of 13¼ miles to the rest huts of Padibei (so called though this place is really some distance away near the Lachit hills). The village is Gweng and the sheikh of the district which is called Kilimanjaro is Agwak. A bugle and drum band met us about two miles out and played the general salute for my benefit, then stayed to play the Uganda people in. As a number of prominent peaks of the Agoro group were visible here, I measured a base and took an azimuth observation in the evening. The people here — Acholi — are nearly all dressed in semi-European clothes and seem a good type. It is a pity to see them discarding their own very picturesque undress and taking to store clothes which are probably never by any chance washed. Powell thought he discovered a case of sleeping sickness in the village here and took a blood slide: unfortunately he could not complete the test as he was short of alcohol and some other indispensables.

Jan. 24th The others left in the morning; Powell staying to do some more doctoring and I to take a round of angles of the hills. I stupidly passed the cool of the morning in working out my previous observations and found when I got to work that the heat of the sun was so strong as to upset the theodolite entirely. I finally took my observations with a waterproof sheet held over me but it was most unlucky that very few of the peaks were visible and these mostly were indistinct.

Powell and I went to look at the village after lunch; it is built very close, the chief's compound being separated from the rest. As in the case of other Acholi villages and of the Madi away from the river, the village was surrounded by a light stockade of bamboo. The people were singularly unafraid, in fact took very little notice of us, though even to their minds there must be something a little astonishing in troops and white men coming from Khartoum and Mombassa to meet here.

We left about 2.45 and had a short march of 7½ miles to the rest huts of Lukung (so called; the village being Guda and the chief Okech); water here from the Nyimwur which we have crossed three times since leaving Lokai.

I decided to halt a day here and then separate to find out a little about the Farajok country and that to the north. I, Huddleston and 20 camel corps will leave the day after tomorrow for Farajok, Obbo and thence on the road to Tarangole; Bruce with Powell and a section of the 12th and Lilley with a section of the KAR will leave the following day to make a complete tour of the Farajok district as far as the Madi chief Meila. Tufnell intends having a look at the people on the ridge near the boundary he proposes and Harman will take a couple of day's tour with a section. We should all be back about the 3rd or 4th of February and meantime supplies can be pushed up to Madial and the 200 Bunyoro porters engaged for us at Masindi and also the OC Madial post can find out something about the country east of there.

Jan. 25th A welcome lie-in-bed. At Tufnell's request, I went to a palaver which he and Postlethwaite were having with Lukung and Agwak's people on the subject of the recent fighting between them. Last night a letter from Aiyelli, Agwak's wakil was received by P., covered with Arabic characters without any meaning. An impertinent verbal message was also received to the effect that if any attempt was made to extract blood money, Agwak would fight. It appears that his people came and burnt one of the Lukung huts and a large number of grain 'gungins' and a touch of humour was given by our finding a gramophone and ***** burnt on the road, apparently the property of Okech. A picket of KAR was put out during the night and I think P. thought we were going to be attacked. However as I have said, in the morning they all came in to have a palaver. Tufnell first told them the usual story about the two governments being one etc. and I then followed suit; it apparently made a considerable impression.

I gave Bruce instructions about haranguing the Farajok chiefs in company with Lilley as I attach importance to the troops of both Governments being seen together.

I heard from Moore that the second 100 Bunyoro porters left Nimule yesterday with grain and as Bruce has arranged with Tufnell to borrow 100 sacks of grain from Agwak; to be repaid at Madial, we shall be well off for supplies, especially if the animals do not take to 'telabun' a little more kindly than they are doing at present.

I went round the lines with Huddleston in the evening; the camels are doing well but the donkeys are looking mostly very thin and poor, so I hope this ten days' rest will do them good. I sent in a report by mail to Clayton[17] regarding my proposed programme.

Jan. 26th   I and Huddleston with 20 camel corps and 30 camels left at 6 am. I have secured an Acholi who knows a little Arabic and have dismissed my Swahili interpreter whose Nubi and bastard Arabic I can hardly understand and he had disobeyed orders in bringing his wives with him. P. will send him back to Nimule, as he is an undesirable to be wandering about the country. Apropos of this, the Swahili who wrote the mock Arabic letter was found yesterday and soundly beaten.

Aiyelli who appeared at the palaver yesterday was very sportsman-like about the matter; he acknowledged that he was drunk and had told the man to write a letter which was certainly not couched in a proper tone, and he said that he himself ought to receive all the punishment — a very unusual attitude for a native.

We found a cleared road and after about 7 miles met Ocheng the chief of Farajok on the road with some of his people, apparently on

---

[17] Sir Reginald Wingate's private secretary. Later *inter alia* he was Chief Secretary in Palestine (1922–25) and High Commissioner for Iraq, where he died in 1929.

his way in to Lukung. They all turned back with us and ran along till we reached a khor with water at about 12 miles where we halted for midday.

I am not attempting an accurate sketch now, as my main object is to get over the ground; I am merely making a rough field book as I go along with distances estimated by pace of the camels. My servant Adam much appreciates riding on a camel instead of wheeling my perambulator wheel as he usually does. I sent a letter back to Bruce to tell him of the water as we had been told there was none as far as Ocheng.

Yesterday evening we opened our trade goods to see which were the most popular amongst these people; all the beads are apparently acceptable especially Zeilan, Nyau and Rowyan, iron wire and fine iron chain, 'tombak' and 'Amerikani' also are popular but they had no use for our 'malod's' or 'kokab's'. One round of iron wire will apparently purchase a sack of grain so that a load of 60 lbs should buy nearly 10,000 lbs of grain which works out at about 6 piastres an ardeb or less.

I made an endeavour through Postlethwaite's Acholi interpreter to find out a little of the connection between these people and our Shilluk's but could arrive at no result. It is evident that whatever connection there may be, it is a distant one, as a couple of Shilluks in the 12th can hardly understand any of the Acholi talk. The Dinkas understand quite as much of it as they do. There is a theory that the aristocracy of the imperial stock made a great 'trek' north through the sudd leaving the peasantry as the forerunners of the Acholi. This is borne out to some extent by the Shilluk tradition of their passage through the Sudd which opened to their canoes on a young warrior throwing himself into the river fully armed, and also by the fact that three of the seven 'Shen's' or branches of the Shilluks are of the royal house and the 'Mek' is found from each in turn. The connection between the Wakavirondo of the Vidnia Nyanza, the Shilluks, Acholi, Dinkas and Nuers and Annuaks would be most interesting to trace, in fact in all this country there is an immense field for ethnological research. I tried my Dabosa vocabulary which I got from Darley on a Karamojo wild man of Tufnell's and found he could apparently understand most of it. The Karamojo, Turkana, Jiwe, Dabosa and possibly also the Latuka talk the same language.

We went on in the afternoon to Ocheng's village and found it only about 4 miles distant. A camping ground had been newly cleared and several new 'bandars' put up and the flour, grain, sheep etc etc we wanted were soon brought in. One of the most comical sights I have ever seen was the drum and bugle band which met us with the General Salute and afterwards played us into camp. The big drummer crossed his sticks in quite the approved style and the buglers relieved each other at intervals when their breath ran out. The bandmaster was the only one who wore a stitch of clothing and he had a tarbush on his head and an old umbrella in his hand. The big drummer gave the words of command, producing quite a good imitation of 'By the left, quick march'. One could not laugh as the whole thing was evidently so deeply serious to them and to Ocheng. The latter, only about 18 years old, seems to have quite a good control over his people who must be fairly numerous as we saw at least a dozen villages of his. He had met us in the road in his everyday attire — a blanket and tarbush, he disappeared soon after we got in, to change into his Sunday clothes of Khaki with solar topee. Many of his people were quite well dressed too.

I put my interpreter '*malgré lui*' in charge of Ocheng as he showed a disposition to return to his own village, but O. appeared after dinner and reported he had run away. However about 11 pm we were woken up by O. arriving with the interpreter, so that the kind words I said to him when he announced the escape had some effect. Unluckily the sky was too cloudy to take a latitude in the evening and the observations I took in the morning before re-starting were also unsatisfactory.

Jan. 27th We got off about 6 am with the interpreter and Ocheng's uncle as a guide. Soon after crossing the Ateipi which was about 1'6" deep over a width of 70', we were met by Burri the chief of the Obbo district, resplendently attired in white drill with a white sun helmet, French boots etc. He also had his band with him which preceded us as far as his village; they were not quite as striking as Ocheng's as some of them were clothed, and they certainly had less idea of tune. It seems that all these chiefs buy the instruments from Ali Dinar at Nimule — the bugles, it was satisfactory to find, came from Gamage's. Burri had only just got news of our visit and had about 100 of his men hard at work clearing a camping ground and building a 'bandar'; I must confess that all these chiefs seem to be imbued much more with the idea of what is due by them to the Government than the majority of ours in the Sudan. It seems that the Obbo people are true Acholi and are practically one with Farajok, they are moreover in close touch with the people of Agwak so it certainly seems unwise to divide them off under the new boundary arrangements.

Between Obbo and the Agoro group of hills there are no inhabitants; Obbo now includes four villages only; having been greatly weakened by repeated raids by the Lokoya and Aiyirri; the latter being the hill tribe near the source of the Gomorro river who were punished by the force under Webb-Bowen last year. To the east of Obbo there is nothing till Payikwara (chief Adur, who is half Acholi, half Madi) is reached. East of this region is Payikeir (chief Meila who is a pure Madi and who controls the people on the Gondokoro road south of the Uma river). There are still three Acholi districts some distance north of Obbo — Agoro (chief Kasiba), Bugwi (chief Ruangau), Umayo (chief Butto); all these drink from the Ayi which is a tributary of the Gomorro. It would be a pity for the Sudan not to get the progressive people of Farajok and Obbo who with their fondness of clothes and such marks of civilisation as brass bands would be worth having, but I fail to see at present how we can cut them off from the remaining Acholi.

After some delay in getting guides, we left Burri's at 9.40 am and marched mostly across country — burnt grass and trees — for an hour and a quarter, when we halted at a pool of water in Khor Burokwach, the water from which eventually finds its way into the Ateipi. Progress is very slow with camels whenever the track is left but it is an enormous advantage to be independent as regards water. I hope we shall be able to get as far as Tarangole one of the chief places of the Latuka which has been mentioned as a possible site for a post. We shall then probably find it equally quick to return to Lukung by the other side of the Agoro hills, parallel to which we are now marching at a distance of about 10 miles. They are a formidable looking range, rising apparently in places to about 9000' above the sea. We went on again at $\frac{1}{2}$ past three and marched mostly through close bush until 5.45, when elephant were reported ahead.

As Huddleston got one before getting into Nimule, I went after them and soon came up with a herd of about 60 scattered about feeding. For a long time I could see nothing but cows and calves but eventually as it was getting dark I saw a bull with tusks about 60 lbs weight. The camel corps askari with me who was carrying my second rifle was rather a nuisance as he got very excited and kept on urging me to shoot. I at last got close to the bull when it was still just light enough to see the sights but just as I was going to fire, he turned tail on and I lost the chance. Finally I had to give it up as it was too dark to see. I got back to camp about seven o'clock and found my interpreter whom I had brought from Agwak's and who had tried to run away last night at Ocheng's, had not yet come in though he had followed us when I went out after the elephant. We lit fires, fired more shots and sounded the bugles at intervals but he did not turn up, though we heard an angry trumpeting from an elephant in answer to our blast of our bugle.

Early in the afternoon I shot a doe waterbuck so it was rather surprising he had not come in to get his chance of the meat.

I was just able to take a couple of observations for latitude before the sky was overcast with the smoke from grass fires.

Jan. 28th We started at 6 am and got to the Khor Ayi which flows into the Gomorro, in ten minutes. Here we had expected to find the missing man but there were no signs of him so H. took a dozen men and scoured the bush for him for an hour without result.

Meantime the guides who had come with us from Obbo told me that he was a 'Miriam' = woman and had a soft heart, that he had run away because he was afraid of the Aiyirri; so altogether I was not upset when we eventually had to start without him, as he knew his way back to Obbo. We had a slow and circuitous morning's march through thick bush and finally crossed the Gomorro at a difficult place at about 10.15 am. Halted here for midday as this is the camels' watering day. All the morning we have seen numerous tracks of elephant; this no-man's land must be full of them. I find my sketch leaves a great deal to be desired in the matter of accuracy but at any rate it will give a better idea of the country than the existing maps which are very imaginative.

We re-started at 2.30 pm and had a very difficult and roundabout march towards the break in the line of hills between J. Kaffai and Lomallo. For the most part we had to cut our way through the jungle with axes, finding out here and there elephant paths to help us a little. After nearly two hours we reached some deserted cultivation and huts of the Aiyirri people who apparently inhabit both the hills just named. The village was roughly but very efficiently stockaded but the huts were of an exceedingly primitive kind — probably the people only come down from the hills for the cultivation season. A number of rough traps to be seen which our guide says are to catch rats.

We finally reached the end of the southern spur of Kaffai at 5.30

and went on another 20 minutes to the watering place of the natives on Khor Kidol, a deep jungle grown watercourse with excellent running water draining North and not to the Gomorro which only takes the tributaries from the western slopes of the hills.

We saw a number of the Aiyirri on the tops of the hill but none ventured down. We had a comparatively clear space to camp, zeriba'd and made a fire. I let off one of Bruce's rockets before we turned in to frighten the people off disturbing us.

Jan. 29th A peaceful night and we re-started at 6 am. For four hours we had a most arduous march down the valley and across the continuous intervening spurs. We had to cut practically all the way; at one spot where we had to descend to the watercourse itself, it looked as if we were going to be absolutely stuck as the jungle on the almost precipitous slope seemed impenetrable. To make matters easier, just as we had cut a path and the camels were sliding carefully down it, an alarm was given that the 'Abied' were coming on us behind; however when H. and I went back, we could see no sign of them.

Finally about 10.15, one of the men spotted some natives on the eastern ridge above the valley — of course making to shoot at them at once in the usual civilising Sudanese way. After a great deal of trouble and shouting, we eventually induced them to come down and found through our very inefficient interpreter that they were the people of a hill called Abili which we could see further down the valley. They had apparently been sent by their sultan to bring us down. They and the people of J. Mukurro whom we saw later are Latuka's in language and by connection, and the Aiyirri are probably just the same. I cannot believe the latter are very numerous or powerful, judging by what we saw of huts on the hills or down below; I suspect that they have acquired a cheap reputation by raiding in small parties the weak Obbo. Soon after these new guides had joined us, we came to cultivation in the valley bed and a path. It is extraordinary what a very short period of pathless march will do to make one appreciate the narrowest and worst footpath.

We finally left the Kidol valley and struck off N.E. soon coming in sight of the distant Latuka range. Passing a pretty village perched on the slopes of J. Mukorro, we finally halted on a small but deep Khor Lomudo which had running water. Here we found the 'Sultan' of Abili — Adiong — who was dressed in clothes, differing from all his people who were stark naked. The 'Sultan' of Mukorro — Leisum —

soon after arrived in a gorgeous embroidered red waistcoat. From this point there is said to be a path to Tarangole in Latuka — there seems frequent communication and the other day Lokeida, the big chief of Latuka, came here to marry a girl. The people here have four sets of radiating cuts (four cuts in each set) on the forehead and another on each cheek. They are mostly small and well built but they are of a distinctly low type. The have a peculiar method of shaking hands — taking the first and second fingers of one's right hand with their own, holding them up a moment as high as possible, then leaving hold with a snap of the fingers.

We re-started about 2.30 but had two delays, one by a camel falling head first into a small khor and having to be unloaded and the second in a very narrow escape for H. — by his camel also making a false step and falling down about 5 feet into a wide pit, H. just getting out of the way of being crushed.

The chief — or rather the son of Abila, as the old man, who apparently has known Baker was too lame to walk, produced a goat, fowls and eggs on the way and was made happy when we got to camp by a red handkerchief, some fine iron chain, a few beads and some tobacco. We took a rather circuitous course above Ene to a Khor Iyodo which has a foot of running water, and finally halted near to it at 6 pm.

30th Jan. The three men who had come with Abila's son took to their heels when day began to break, and the latter was strolling off with the casual remark that he was going to the water when I had him taken charge of. It seems there's a feud between Abila's and the people of Killio, the next village ahead and they were rather afraid of approaching the latter too nearly. We were obliged to take the man along for an hour till we reached a path, led by a leather camel rope but let him go then with the additional present of a whistle from H. We had a difficult pass over a low range of hills to cross in the extremity of the Killio group and then lost some time in doing so, having to cut a path, but the interval was utilised in calling to the people on the hill to come down which they finally did, accompanied by a man who had apparently been sent by Lokeida the chief of Tarangole to show us the way.

Still no path except occasional elephant tracks through the high grass till we came to a difficult watercourse the Giyaneta which flows north and the water of which in flood season reaches the Veveno in

PLATE 1

Captain Harry Kelly, Royal Engineers (1880–1914).

PLATE 2

Escort leaving Mongalla (probably January 3rd). Soldiers in the foreground belong to the 12th Sudanese. Owen's 'police band' which played them down to the landing place can be seen in the centre.

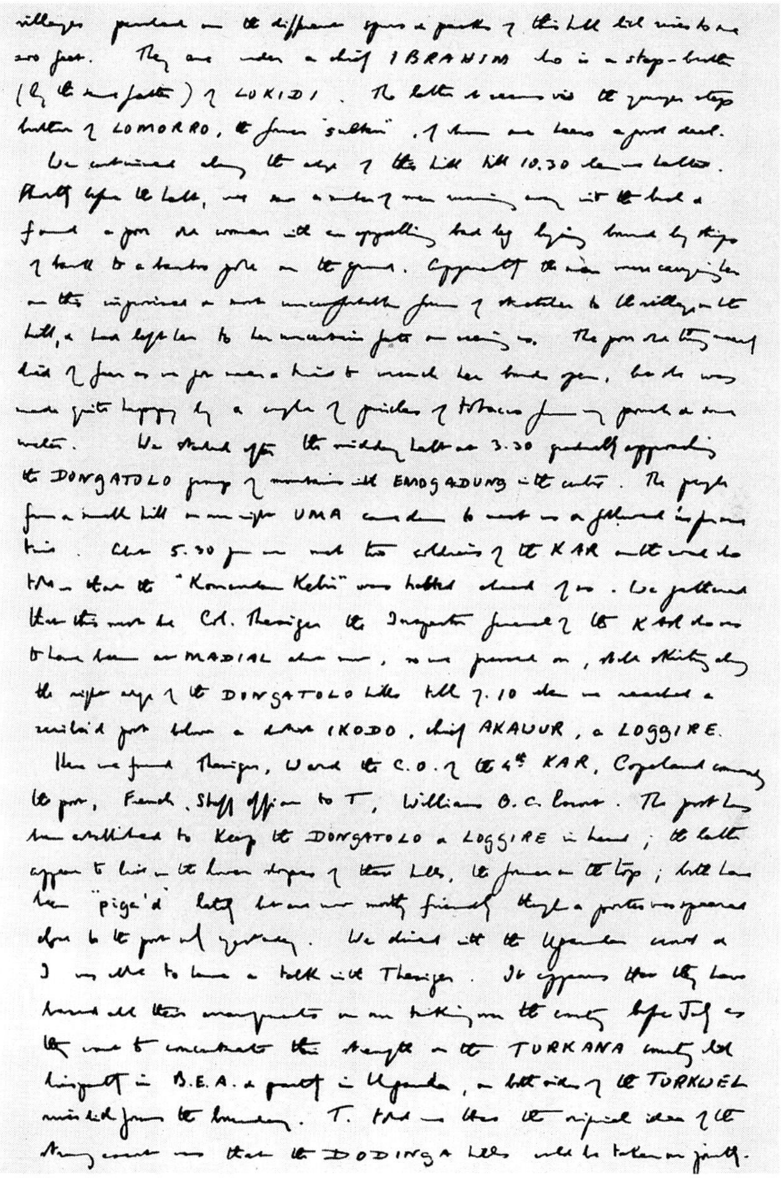

Diary entry February 2nd.
We dined with the Ugandan crowd and I was able to have a talk with Thesiger. It appears that they have based all their arrangements on our taking over the country before July as they want to concentrate their strength on the Turkana country which lies partly in B. E. A. and partly in Uganda, on both sides of the Turkwell river which forms the boundary.

PLATE 4

Group at Nimule, assembled at the start of the Commission to discuss the boundary. Back row: probably six Egyptian officers. Middle row left to right: Postlethwaite, Anderson, Bruce, Weatherhead. Front row left to right: Lilley, Kelly, Mrs Anderson, Tufnell.

the Beir country. Both near this khor and yesterday on the Iyodo we saw a few 'fly'. We halted near here for midday in a spot which was soon cleared by our following from Killio. The latter are quite stark naked as are the people of Abili and have the same face marks as the latter. They however have quite a different form of greeting, coming up and passing their right hand twice over the face as if they were washing. They appeared to be perfectly unsophisticated and were delighted with a handkerchief, an empty rocket-cartridge and a few zeilan beads in exchange for a sheep and a large bowl of flour. So pleased indeed were they that they afterwards brought a kid and more flour in exchange for two empty 303 cartridge cases and a quantity of 'ful Sudani' for a few beads — a cheap country to live in at present. In the afternoon we made good progress with the guides from Killio, getting very successfully over a difficult looking pass over a low range of hills (for which I got several names, possibly Kilikili being the correct one and I found that Angarama mentioned on the old maps is the name of the col only, in the same way as Lomudo, the name of the place we crossed the Giyaneta was given us as the name of the river itself). From Angarama we had a wonderful view over the plains towards the Latuka hills, into which we now descended. A beautiful afternoon, a well wooded plain with good going in spite of the lack of a path, and a magnificent view of the Latuka hills in front and the Lugwire group, with Imatong towering up, to the right rear.

Many traces of elephant on the plain as there also were near the Giyanetta and at the Angarama pass where the path had been entirely made by them. We saw a number of Jackson hartebeest and oribi but Huddleston who dismounted could not get a shot. It looks as if Tarangole would be an ideal place for a station judging from its situation and should be healthy as the soil is everywhere of a firm sandy nature except for a width of some 600 yards in the middle of the plain where there is a shallow water course.

31st Jan.   A very hot night, the first since leaving Nimule. Started at 6 am. H. went in front to try and shoot something and about 7 came back to say he had seen a rhino, so we both got heavy rifles and went after it. After ½ an hour we saw it — a cow with a calf. They got our wind and came across our front at a fast trot. H. had won the toss for first shot — I never by any chance win this, so I waited before I heard what I thought was his shot before I fired twice. The rhinos went off quickly, H. firing as they went. We found the calf about 300 yards away standing over the big one. It refused to be chased away and tried to come for us so I had to shoot it, which was unpleasant. The old one was shot through the lungs and practically dead. H. then told me that the animal was mine as his rifle had missed fire and the shot I heard was one of the two askaris who were following us and who could not restrain his feelings — he was the same man who tried to shoot the friendly people from Abili whom we saw on the hill the day before yesterday. When the rest of the men came up, they fell on the animal at once to get pieces of hide to make sandals and 'Kurbags'. I found the top of the skull with the horns came away quite easily and that there is an entrance to the brain just below the big horn for a frontal shot which I did not know. The heart we found to be about 12 inches by 14 situated just behind the point of the shoulder, rather lower than half way up the body. We took the four feet as trophies and the men loaded themselves with meat. We saw a good deal of game afterwards, roan, tiang, hartebeest, oribi, dijdij, bustard. A wide patch of cotton soil with bad going and only scattered thorn trees in the centre of the valley, then sandy soil again with close thorn bush, a good deal of 'hashab' to be seen which will be a useful asset if ever there is a post in these parts. We reached a considerable village at 11.30 and escorted by numbers of the people — all quite naked — went on across Khor Kos, a dry sandy bed 60' wide, over a plain of firm sandy soil well wooded with haqlij, hashab, seyal and ardeib. Half a mile before reaching Tarangole we were met by the chief Lokedi who was dressed in Khaki with a polo hat — a very evil face with a bad squint. We halted outside the village at the rest huts which were in bad condition. Water from Khor Kos about [?] away, where water is obtained by digging. I explained to Lokedi who we were — though it was apparently no news to him that we came from Khartoum. The chief 'sultans' of the Latuka are himself, Tofeng (a woman) at J. Abalo some twelve miles west of here, Achaleli at Loronyo, Isara near Okela, Lojedo who is the chief of the hill people who keep to themselves. Lokidi told us that no one from the Government had been here and that there was a good deal of trouble amongst the 'abied' owing to the non-existence of government. His own people fight continually with Achaleli's. There is apparently a cleared road from here to Luromo which seems to be the same place as Madial or close to it. As usual much difficulty owing to not having an efficient interpreter; I cannot make out where we branch off from this main road to get back to Lukung. This seems a remarkably good position for a station, an open site on sandy soil, fine ranges of hills in three directions as a view, probably good water from Khor Kos, a big centre of population, pleasant wooded country around, abundant game and apparently no fly, as there are cattle to be seen here. With luck I ought to be able to fix this place exactly as there is a good view of the pointed peak Lodio in the Latuka hills, which was fixed by Pearson last year.[18]

1st Feb. I took a sun azimuth yesterday evening but unluckily found that the theodolite I have with me — number two — differs 6 minutes in the readings of the two horizontal viewers, so the round of angles I took will not be very accurate. I also took several latitude operations later, so shall be able to get a fair fixing for this place from J. Lodio. A hot night. This morning I took two more sets of azimuth observations and after breakfast H. and I went to look at the town with Lokidi. It covers an area of about 600 yards by 150 and is closely built; each compound is stockaded — rather inefficiently. The houses are of mud with a high conical roof extending nearly down to the ground. A new and large hut was being built for Lokidi himself; the roof was built upside down, the cone top being let into the ground, the fellakebs being bound to a height of about 8 feet on the 25′ long bamboo 'rafters'. Perhaps for our benefit, the operation of putting the roof on the hut walls was done while we were there. About 80 men got around the roof, raised it out of its seating in the ground, turned it over and with the help of long forked branches and of men standing on the walls of the hut, upended it and seated it on the hut, the completed portion being still well above the walls and the weight being carried by the bamboos resting on the walls all round.

We asked to see the 'Kujur' or witch doctor who proved to be a very retiring savage. The office descends from father to son but his duties extend to curing the sick and providing charms, and do not cover rain making. We asked to see his medicine which proved to be a piece of wood for chewing. He also produced a charm against enemies — a worn piece of wood 2″ long with a hole in it. The men are all naked and are of a distinctly low type. The women are even uglier, wear tattered skins as a kilt and mostly have a cylinder of wood an inch in length and diameter through a hole in the lower lip.

The men here have not as a rule the broad arrow markings on the

---

[18] Hugh Pearson was Director of Surveys of Sudan government survey department from 1904 until his death in 1922.

face and it would seem that the people of Abili are distinct from them and speak a dialect, similar to that of Imatong but understandable by the Latuka. Lokidi produced a bull as a present last night, a thousand lbs of red dhurra besides a sheep, chickens etc. On request he also brought a brass helmet, most ingeniously made on a basis of human hair with longitudinal strips of brass 2″ wide — hammered out of brass wire — covering most of it, also a shield of buffalo hide about 4′6″ long and 2′ wide. He wanted to make us a present of these. He has quite a number of cattle at least 30 grown animals, and says there is no fly here now.

Somewhere in the vicinity of this place would be an excellent place for a station, it is only about 100 miles from Rejaf, the road to which would run through Belinian, Liria, Lokoya, Abalo. There is 'hashab' gum as well as some 'belk' in the neighbourhood, sim-sim (sesame) could, judging by the crops in the Acholi and Madi country, be grown in quantities, and probably cotton would grow well in the lower ground to the west. The quality of dhurra is good, so that the ground is evidently fertile.

The town of Tarangole itself is not well situated being on rather low ground, the site of the rest huts is higher but the ground road will be wet in the rains. Lokidi however has a number of villages, probably at least six, and near one of these, a good site could no doubt be found on firm sandy soil. At Kaburira, the village we passed about a mile back yesterday, for instance could be a good site. It would make an excellent centre to administer the Latuka speaking people, including Lafit (chief Lojedo) and Boya (who are hostile to the Latuka). I am as yet no nearer finding a suitable Acholi-Latuka boundary as the hill people of Aggoro are very mixed. I expect the boundary proposed by the Uganda people will prove the best, but J. Sereteinia certainly is Acholi or Lango and should go to them.

We gave Lokidi a miscellaneous collection as a return for the bull, 1,000 lbs of grain, shield, helmet, fowls etc. — an old Thermos flask belonging to H., a bandanna handkerchief, three soldiers' handkerchiefs, 6 rounds of iron wire, a lb of tobacco, some thin iron chain and 11 rupees — he seemed very pleased so we were all satisfied. We started at 2.30 pm and found an excellent road surface, thoroughly cleared to 4 metres width, so got along well. After 8 miles through very pleasant country with a great deal of 'hashab' gum we reached the hill of Logguren where on the steep rocky slopes is scattered a village which is under Lokidi, water from holes in Khor Koss ¼ mile away. This seemed an excellent site, better from most points of view than Tarangole, being on firm sandy soil with a good slope down to the khor, along which are large numbers of 'doleib' palms which make the outlook very pleasant. A closer and better view of the Imatong and Agoro range as well as of the fantastic looking Dongatolo group. The Boya hills (people called Irengi) are visible over a wooded plain some 30 miles east, so this would make a good centre.

There were a few cattle to be seen so that fly is not to be feared, and the forest around is delightfully pretty. The people came down in numbers from the hill and were very friendly. We did another 5½ miles, still with excellent going which both men and camels must have appreciated after our recent wanderings across thick country, and halted at a deserted village Oliunga, ½ mile from Khor Koss; still many palms everywhere. The two guides from Lokidi proved quite intelligent, but the information which I gained from them regarding the various hill people makes the question of frontiers more complex than ever. The Imatong people talk a language resembling Latuka and have been to Tarangole to salute Lokidi, but they mostly stay on their hills and are not by any means pure Latuka — probably an Acholi mixture.

On the lower slopes of Imatong are three Latuka villages under a chief Lokorinyan who is subject to Lokidi. The hill people of Dongatolo who inhabit the hills around J. Egadung and are called Loggire on the map and not so in reality, are of the Lango extraction and talk that language, as do more or less the Loggire people who are on the west of these hills and also on the range south of Imatong.

2nd Feb. A hot night again. Started at 6 am, passed a village Hadessik which is under Lokidi and crossing the Koss twice, got to J. Lopi or Lofi at 9.20, good going on a cleared road nearly all the way. There are two or three villages perched on the different spurs and peaks of this hill which rises to some 200 feet. They are under a chief Ibrahim who is a step-brother (by the same father) of Lokidi. The latter it seems is the younger step brother of Lomorro, the former 'sultan', of whom one hears a good deal.

We continued along the edge of this hill till 10.30 when we halted. Shortly before the halt, we saw a number of men running away into the bush and found a poor old woman with an appalling bad leg lying bound by strips of bark to a bamboo pole on the ground. Apparently the men were carrying her on this improvised and most uncomfortable form of stretcher to the village on the hill, and had left her to her uncertain fate on seeing us. The poor old thing nearly died of fear as we got near and tried to wrench her bonds open, but she was made quite happy by a couple of pinches of tobacco from my pouch and some water. We started after the midday halt at 3.30 gradually approaching the Dongatolo group of mountains with Emogadung in the centre. The people from a small hill on our right Uma came down to meet us and followed us for some time. About 5.30 pm we met two soldiers of the KAR on the road who told us that the 'Kommander Kebir' was halted ahead of us. We gathered that this must be Colonel Thesiger the Inspector General of the KAR who was to have been at Madial about now, so we pressed on, still skirting along the right edge of the Dongatolo hills till 7.10 when we reached a zeriba'd post below a distant Ikodo, chief Akawur, a Loggire. Here we found Thesiger, Ward the CO of the 4th KAR, Copeland commanding the post, French, Staff Officer to T., Williams OC Escort. The post has been established to keep the Dongatolo and Loggire in hand; the latter appear to live on the lower slopes of these hills, the former on the top; both have been 'piga'd' lately but are now mostly friendly though a porter was speared close to the post only yesterday. We dined with the Ugandan crowd and I was able to have a talk with Thesiger. It appears that they have based all their arrangements on our taking over the country before July as they want to concentrate their strength on the Turkana country which lies party in BEA and partly in Uganda, on both sides of the Turkwel river which forms the boundary. T. told me that the original idea of the strong escort was that the Dodinga hills would be taken on jointly. He was strongly of the opinion that there should be no interregnum which would allow the stronger tribes to make reprisals on the weaker who had helped the Government.

He was quite ready to take on the Dodinga with three companies but the Uganda Government could not find the necessary funds £4000. We ourselves could certainly not do the job so cheaply and since the opportunity has now been lost of subduing this tribe jointly, I think it would pay us to let the Ugandan people do the 'piga-ing' at our expense, if we do not take over in the near future. As T. is going home via Jondokoro, he will see the Sirdar and be able to explain this to him.

3rd Feb.   Rain fell for ½ an hour at 4.30 am and we were delayed in going off in clearing up our camp and by the disappearance of our two guides who were eventually led in by a couple of soldiers we sent after them. They said they had been to fetch in the chief Ibrahim who was camped near and who followed them, so they got off cheaply with 6 light lashes. I should have been sorry to lose them as they were both intelligent. We finally left about 7 am and stopped half an hour later to water the camels and fill waterskins which occupied till 8.30. We now left the well cleared main road which goes on to Madial and struck on to a native path through thorn bush towards the E. side of Tereteinia. Having once cleared the last of the outlying hills of Dongatolo, we came into what I should imagine was typical East African country, grass 4' high with sparse thorn bush.

Far away to the east could be seen the long Dodinga range while to the S.E. was the Nyangeir group at the north of which Madial is — only about 27 miles from the Loggire post. We halted at 11 am after about ten miles, as we had done a good day's march yesterday of about 27 miles. Restarted at 3.30 pm, striking in towards the northern extension of J. Logila which is itself that of Tereteinia. The track led through thick thorn bush, which in places made riding impossible. We were joined by Lokumamoi the chief of Logila, the huts of which are perched on the hill side. Halted at 6.40 pm below Tereteinia with a fine view to the east. There seems to be a clearly defined southern end to the Dodinga hills so the boundary there should present no difficulties. A number of people came in from the hill during the evening with sheep etc. The people of these hills are distinctly Lango which is a tribe closely akin to Acholi.

4th Feb. Started at 6.10, and more or less hugged the bottom of the hills for an hour and a half to a rest camp, just before which we met the main road to Madial. Here we found a number of Bunyoro porters returning from M. — these are probably the men carrying our supplies out. The water supply here was very poor being contained in a small 'haifir' and being very dirty. The natives of the place (chief Lomeya) say it fills up quickly after being emptied and I told him to dig out all round so as to increase its capacity before our return in a few days.

Apparently the main road from here goes south of east under a pointed hill Madi, but we were taken by a path which proved very little better than what we had yesterday. We cleared the last of Tereteinia by 10 o'clock and struck out across the plain towards the Agoro range, the highest point of which seems to be J. Tiya. From our halting place at 11 am, there appears a clear valley between this range and the northern extension of Tereteinia, so it seems as if it might be well if

we take Agoro, to give T. to Uganda as being Lango and allied to their
people in the south, although the Loggire also talk the same language
and should by rights also go to Uganda.[19] The people of Tiya are
Acholi-Lango while those of Imatong to the north are more Latuka
than anything else. A strictly tribal boundary would probably therefore
cut between these two main peaks but such in practice would be quite
unworkable as the whole group is more or less one mass. Unless I find
there is a very clearly marked gap between Lalak and Lamwa, I am
inclined to think the only practical solution would be for us to take
the whole of the Agoro group and even perhaps include Agwak and
his Acholi.

In the afternoon we had a march of 2¾ hours over more open
country for the most part, though the thorn bush was thick here and
there, to Aggoro, which consists of two large Acholi valleys (chief
Lumoi) under a small hill which apparently lends the name under
which the whole group goes. There is good running water here in Khor
Okora which runs south to join Khor Arenga and eventually joins the
Assua. An excellent open camping ground and a pretty view round
with fine gemeiza trees and the so-called 'park-like' haqlij country.
Lumoi is an intelligent Arabic speaking man and brought everything
we asked for quickly. We found 96 porters here carrying 'wimbi' and
'matama' to Madial from Nimule for our use; as I did not know for
certain if Harman had all the grain he wanted for the transport
onwards, I sent a couple of runners to Tufnell who we heard was at
Palanga the next post, to ask.

5th Feb. A four hour march mostly along a cleared road brought us
to Palanga which lies on Khor Arenga which has running water. Here
we found Tufnell and Warner; Postlethwaite and Lilley arrived later.
We had a long discussion about the boundary, Tufnell wanting to carry
it along the ridge overlooking the valley between here and Aggu, the
hill near Lukung. His idea in this was to give Uganda the Acholi who
live on the lower slopes of these hills and who, according to P., are
administered. There is much to be said for this as our Inspectors at
Tarangole and Kajo-Kaji would not be well placed for running these
people who would moreover continue in close connection with the

---

[19] In this instance, Kelly's view on tribal boundaries was not correct. In September 1926 an
area of the Tereteinia foothills was transferred from Sudan to Uganda in an effort to reunite
the Lango people.

Acholi further south, thus causing possible difficulties if they were separated. I objected to an indefinite frontier which might or might not prove a true tribal one but T. insisted that there are no Acholi north of his proposed line.

Their contention is not altogether logical, for Farajok and Obbo are as truly Acholi as any one else and are in close connection with Agwak's and Lukung whilst the people of Palwar on the west side of the hills north of Aggu are also Acholi. However they insist that this will cause no difficulty and I am now disposed to accept their idea as the people of F. and O. will be very useful to us if we ever come to build the railway from Gondokoro to Nimule. Tufnell was much upset when I said that if we could not come to a definite conclusion based on knowledge and not on supposition regarding the hill Acholi, I must delay ten days or a fortnight in these parts to solve the question. It is unfortunate that he is so anxious to rush the whole affair — as he goes on leave directly it is finished, and I also am beginning to feel that the burden of finding out all information tending to settle the boundary is lying with me, in addition to the work of mapping it. I started off again at 2.30 pm with six camels, following the south side of the gap in the hills. The road was only cleared in parts though parties of Acholi were at work on it. About 4, heavy rain came on, making progress difficult for the camels. I met Bruce about a mile outside the Amaiyo camp. He and Powell had had a very successful trip through Farajok and made a useful map which defines the limits and makes it possible to decide a line there. Powell found what he thinks is a decided case of sleeping sickness in Palwar; forty of this village had died during the last three years of the same mysterious complaint, whatever it was. They were very well received everywhere, got plenty of food for their porters and at Farajok Ocheng's brought 100 sacks of grain for the transport.

I had a shivering fit when I got in from my wetting but was put more or less right by a hot whiskey and water; though I had some fever in the night. I heard that Tufnell and Warner had during our absence been up on the hill and burnt out several villages for the reason that they wanted the people to live on the lower ground so as to be more accessible — which somewhat naturally they were unwilling to do. The Uganda system is quite contrary to ours in the Sudan, very decidedly on the 'fortiter in modo' plan.[20] Whatever may be said

[20] See Note 14.

of the means, the result is unquestionably good for the people do all they are required to do, clear their roads at frequent intervals, produce supplies and are apparently very pleased to see one which is a good test. The Acholi are certainly a good race and with opportunity would certainly be progressive for they have all the instincts which tend to progress. Their chiefs must I think have considerable influence over their immediate followers judging by what one can see. As a rule they are a fine looking lot of men — most wear the curious small conical top knot composed of hair crowned by a cartridge case, many have a ⌒ shaped piece of glass through a hole in the lower lip — this is ground down from pieces of bottle I believe. Tattooing is general but not on any fixed plan. Many men wear a kind of cummerbund composed of dozens of strands of coarse string. The women are generally very ugly, they wear either an apron of tanned hide or a diminutive sporran made of lengths of thin chain.

I told Harman to go on to Madial in any way he thinks best but that he would probably find it well to stop by Aggoro till I come.

6th Feb. Bruce and I started at 7 am, the escort having left earlier. A nine mile march through the valley to the Khor Nyimwur where we halted at a village; I left the sketching to the return journey. We did the remaining six miles into Lukung in the afternoon, heavy rain having fallen meantime. I sketched the latter part as tomorrow I want to leave Lukung in time to climb Aggu by about 8 am, so as to be able to take a sun azimuth. At Lukung I was amused by the little chief Achama a boy of about three years old coming out from the village by himself to shake me by the hand, encouraged by the people of the village. The people here are pretty badly off now, as they had about fifty tons of grain burnt by Agwak's people in the recent dispute, during which three people were killed on either side. It struck me that the people were very surprised to be paid in beads for the grain and flour they brought in — this seems to be contrary to their usual experience.

7th Feb. Bruce and I left Lukung at 4.45 with the cook and a few carriers with theodolite and breakfast, as I was anxious to get azimuth observations from Aggu. However after half an hour rain came on and continued hard till late in the afternoon rendering it quite impossible to see any hills. The hamla arrived at 10.30 am; Bruce and I had meantime made ourselves comfortable in the village where we halted at midday yesterday, getting a hut-roof raised on improvised supports as a shelter. The people were apparently very pleased to see us and made a hut for the men in the afternoon. We went for a short walk in the evening and found a number of villages near, all roughly stockaded with bamboo and provided with the usual 'club' outside — a raised seat with shelter over where the men sit most of the day. I passed the afternoon working out observations — making numbers of arithmetical mistakes as usual.

Given good weather I think I should be able to get accurate results from now on as Pearson fixed a high hill about 20 miles from Madial to the N.E. which should be visible for a considerable distance after leaving Tereteinia. I got a note from Harman sending my map case which I had asked for and telling me three of the camels which came out with me and Huddleston had died. I know two were sick so I am hoping this is not the beginning of a heavy mortality from 'fly' as those two had coughs. We shall be very dependent on camels later on unless sufficient rain falls to make considerable rain pools.

8th Feb. A moderately fine dawn so Bruce and I started off for the ascent of Agu at 6.20 with a couple of porters carrying theodolite boxes and a number of Acholi as guides and carrying odds and ends. We took a rather roundabout route, reached the beginning of the stiff climb at 7.30 but did not reach the top (as seen from camp) till 9.15. This proved not to be the actual highest point which was about 100' higher but was then fixed by me from Agwak's. The climb was difficult being nearly all through bamboo; luckily most of the grass was burnt as in the parts where it was not, it was almost impassable. By the time I had my theodolite set up, it would have been too late to take a sun azimuth which I was not sorry for, as I found I had no blue glass eyepiece to the telescope so could not have done one in any case! However I had fixed Agu and Lalak so could use them as a reference line.

There was an excellent view from the top, in fact Otze the mountain far west of Nimule was quite distinct; the view probably covered well over 100 miles. The Ilala hills at the south of the 'Agoro' group closed the view to Tereteinia but I think Harogo which was fixed by Pearson was visible. I took a good double round of angles and by the time I had identified the hills in Farajok which Bruce had picked out and got packed up ready to descend, it was after 12. We went back to our village by a direct line, rather precipitous in places through thick bamboo and grass, finally reaching the village about 2.45. The actual height above camp of the climb was about 2700 so we did a good morning's work. I had sent on the escort (2 NCOs and 6 men) and mule transport in the morning and had only some dates in my saddle bag, so was very glad to find Bruce had been more provident and had prepared a tin of soup and some bread. The sky looked very threatening so I had to hurry off to try and get my sketch through before it began to rain. Fortunately the storm only just touched us and though we got a bit wet, I was able to get in the line of hills along the route all right, though to be sure only approximately. I reached camp at Amaiya's at 6 pm rather tired and very hungry. It is certainly a very pleasant site being well cleared, less than — mile from the almost sheer hillside and on the bank of the deep watercourse where the Nyimwur which we have crossed so many times begins its course.

We were getting a little anxious about the two Buganda porters who were carrying the theodolite boxes and whom we had left to come down Agu with Amaiya the chief of this place and two Acholi — especially as after Tufnell piga'ing the people about here, two unarmed porters might be speared. However they finally rolled up safely with Amaiya about 7.30 pm. Rain threatened again in the evening; I hope it will ultimately benefit us as regards water supply as it is decidedly unpleasant and inconvenient now.

9th Feb.   A beautiful morning and marching was a real pleasure, it is wonderful how the rain had freshened up everything. We had intended to divide the distance to Palonga into two but Bruce who was ahead overshot the water so we went right through about 13 miles. I spent the rest of the day in getting on with the plotting of my map which has got much behindhand. The sky was overcast till about 7.30 pm but then cleared a little, so I took an azimuth in order to get a round of angles tomorrow — this place being well situated in view of Lalak, Lamwa, Tereteinia and Madi. After dinner however when I wanted to take a latitude, the sky clouded over again so I had to give it up.

10th Feb.   Bruce, as always full of energy, got up before 4 to see if the stars were up sufficiently for us to observe but found the sky still heavy. An hour after, he called me again and I managed to get some observations. Before leaving camp, I took a round of angles. A march of 13½ miles to Lumoi's where Huddleston and I were before; rain fell on the way but not heavily. Here we found all our people and Tufnell. Postlethwaite, Lilley and Warner had gone up the hills to commence disarming arrangements of the Acholi. I took the opportunity to tell Tufnell that I was sorry that the arrangement made by me with Anderson at Nimule that no punitive measures should be taken while we were about had not been adhered to. Both at Afoka's and here there has been burning if not slaying. T. told me that Yom the man who had been sent from Madial to bring the Dodinga chiefs in, had returned there but had been tied up for several days, during which time the Dodinga raided a further 1500 head of cattle from Morongole. This makes the situation for me all the more difficult. From a common sense point of view, there is no question that this should be punished and moreover that it should be done at once when we have both troops here.

On the other hand my instructions do not permit of my doing anything unless absolutely forced and I am sure that I should not be supported if I took action and anything untoward happened. I cannot help feeling convinced that the Uganda people have taken advantage of our presence to enforce their orders with the Acholi — both at Lukung in the fining of Agwak's people for their raids, in the case of Afoka's where the people were driven off the hill and their huts burnt and here, where the disarming has been ordered to take place immediately.

I spent the rest of the day getting on with my map which goes well but slowly as the hills take a great deal of putting in. Huddleston sent on some of his men to Tereteinia in the afternoon to look after the water supply there, preparatory to the force marching tomorrow. Tufnell seedy as he has been daily for some time; it is a pity that Uganda should have sent a man who, however keen and well suited he is, can have no other idea but leave after nearly 2 year's continual hard trekking.

11th Feb. The escort went off early — I enjoyed a longer morning. Spent the rest of the day getting my map up to date and in working out observations. Agreed finally with Tufnell regarding the boundary up to this — Nimule up the Unyama to J. Ebijo, across to J. Kadomera, down the Assua to Lokai, N.E. over uninhabited country to J. Matoko (leaving this to Uganda), cross the Farajok-Lukung road south east of Khor Laparra, to J. Aggu, thence over the mountains to Ilala and Tiya, leaving to Uganda all the Acholi on the southern and eastern slopes of the range, cross north of Tereteinia to the southern outlying hill of Dongatolo (south of J. Mommo).

I talked over the question of the Dodinga with him; I quite appreciate his point of view and think it a great pity that now we have the troops here we should not punish them for their repeated raids, more especially as the last raid was a pure act of defiance. However my instructions, which I showed him, are so precise that I can do nothing. There is moreover the point of view to be considered that Egyptian troops could not be used in a country that is still a British protectorate to take up the cudgels for the protectorate authorities. Finally I agreed that, as we shall not necessarily be going through Dodinga, Clothier the OC Madial Post should go and take them on at once, provided it is understood that we cannot take any part at all unless we are actually attacked.

Tufnell now thinks we shall be able to get through to Morongole and thence to Zingote which appears to be what we call Tirano; if we can manage this, we shall have completed the mission.

12th Feb. We left Postlethwaite and Fowke (KAR who came over with a company from Madial yesterday) about to start a drive of the Acholi with the object of their complete disarmament.[21] A march of 14½ miles to Tereteinia rest house, much improved by the clearing done since our last visit. I managed to get up to date with my map in the afternoon except for the Latuka journey.

The inferior water in the water holes here was eked out by a supply carried down from the hill by the natives — who appear to be Lango as are the Logire.

13th Feb. A long march over the plains to Madial post — 16½ miles — temper none too good owing to the Shawish of my escort waking us up nearly half an hour late for the stars I wanted to observe this morning. Found the rest of the 'army' comfortably established at Madial, also Clothier and Wilkinson of the KAR and Owen, medical officer. I was relieved yesterday greatly by Tufnell producing a headman of Clothier's as interpreter — he is a Muscat Arab, knows Swahili, Karamojo and a little Amharic, a thorough scoundrel and an ex-dependent of Darley's but a tremendous acquisition as he knows all the country as well as being a linguist.

---

[21] Barber gives some remarkable details about the availability of weapons among the Acholi. In February 1911 a DC had seen 500 firearms and estimated that a further 1200 were owned by the Acholi. Many of these were Gras rifles. (Barber, 1968, p. 108).

In the cool of the afternoon we all went up to a col in the hills behind the post, partly for a view to the east and partly to see if the path would be practicable for camels and thus save us going all round the N. end of the Nyangiya hills to get eastward. A very stiff climb of about 1200 feet, quite impossible even for unloaded camels, but we were rewarded by a good view over the Kideppo valley towards Dodinga.

Tufnell has I am glad to find given up the idea of going for the Dodinga tribe and was glad to fall in with my suggestion that I should do all the reconnaissance for J. Morongole to the north and that he should meet me at M. at the end, and then go south through Karamojo on leave — which he is badly in need of.

3

Interlude in Madial

February 14th–February 16th

Time is spent resting, procuring stores (especially grain) and in local reconnaissance. Kelly agrees with Tufnell that he should go on leave. They agreed to make out a final report on the boundary as soon as possible. This appears to have been concluded during discussions on February 16th. There is increasing concern about the camels, 13 of whom have already died.

14th Feb. I delighted the heart of Laing the old man I picked up at Lumoi's, took to Lukung and up to J. Aggu with the present of a shirt. He was quite an amusing character with a fund of dry humour; in the middle of the steepest part of the Aggu ascent he turned to me and Bruce and asked if there were no hills in Khartoum. When we said no, he said 'Oh, I suppose then you are doing this, so as to be able to go back and tell people that you have been up a real hill'.

I interviewed a number of local worthies to find out about the route to the East; very much lying both on the part of my new interpreter Khamis — who, as a result of a heavy beating which he got today as a punishment for a week's absence without leave, was inclined to take an optimistic view of everything so as to give pleasure — and on the part of the natives who were bent on taking us the round about road to Morongole by the south end of Nyangiya instead of striking across. The reason of this may be that the latter road is used by them in their raids with the Dodinga on the Dodosi or that they are afraid to take us anywhere near the Dodinga. Finally with the assistance of Tufnell, we arrived at a possible three day's route to Morongole, and a way from there to Zulia to the north which should be about the boundary.

Powell was hard at work all the morning in examining the blood of the camels; fifteen have died so far from mysterious causes. He found five were affected by trypanosomes, so no doubt the ones that died had them too. They were mostly the animals which were with H. and me on the Latuka trip where there was a good deal of fly, and it

PLATE 5

Owen and Powell on the march to Nimule (between 7th and 14th March). Owen was the Governor of Mongala Province and Powell the Medical officer accompanying the Commission and escort.

PLATE 6

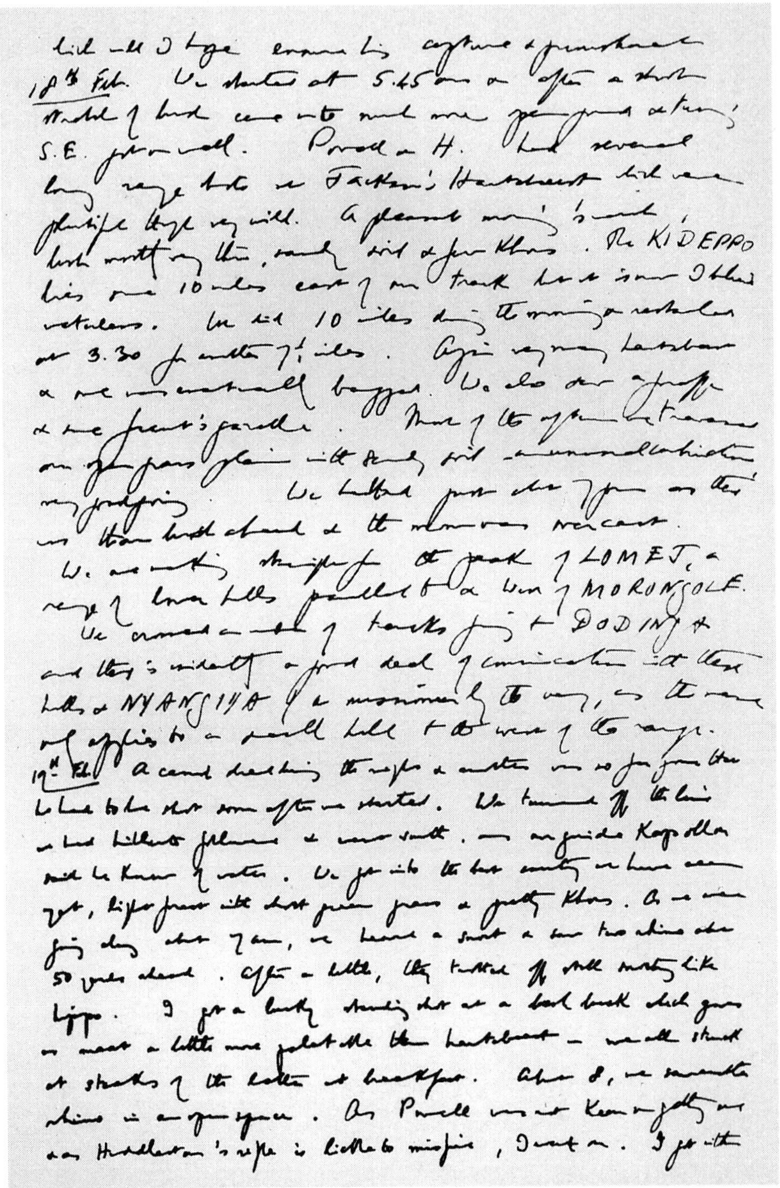

Diary entry February 18th–19th.

Most of the afternoon we traversed over open grass plain with sandy soil, an unusual combination very good going. We halted just about 7 pm as there was thorn bush ahead and the moon was overcast.

PLATE 7

Bruce and Lilley buying flour.

PLATE 8

Morongole camp (possibly February 22nd).
We had a very cold night but enjoyed enormously sitting over a big fire with hot rum and milk after dinner. The natives brought in plenty of milk and wood last night and a couple of sheep and in the morning began bringing in a few 'garrah's' of 'dhurra'.

is noteworthy that those which H. and I rode — always in front — and that of the Onbashi who rode in front of me, all have symptoms.

Tufnell was told by the porters who went to Morongole from here with iron wire to buy grain for us (they only succeeded in buying six bags so far) that Yom, the local go-between with the Dodinga, had been seen with the raiders who went from the latter to M. quite recently. If this is so, he must be a rascal of some resource, for he came back from D. having been sent there to bring the chiefs in to see us, to say that he had been tied up there for several days while the D. went to M., raided 1200 cattle; the D. according to him then told him that he could go back and tell the Government that this raid would show how much they, the D. cared for the Government.

15th Feb. Tufnell, I, Harman and Bruce started at 6.30 am to climb to Mening. About 2 miles to the commencement of the ascent then 1700 feet rise, partly very steep, arriving at rest hut near a spring at 9.45. The people have all been cleared off the hill and made to build below; very hard luck this, I think, as they showed their wisdom in living where they could graze their cattle and be high up. On top, the going was easy, the view close by very pretty whilst as soon as one got a clear outlook, the view in all directions was magnificent. Bruce went up by himself before lunch to the peak 800′ higher than the rest hut and was threatened by some natives who not unnaturally after the treatment of them, were apt to take reprisals if they could. In the afternoon he and I went up about 3.30 with carriers for the night. I shot a Klipspringer with a fluke standing shot about 150 yards. The wind was too strong for me to take any observations in the afternoon but Tufnell and Harman came up later, and I settled with the former a general line from the south of the Logire hills to the east. They went down before dark and we settled down for the night with a guard of 4 men of the KAR Luckily we were more or less sheltered and though a very strong wind was blowing from the east, we had quite a strong west wind as a back blast. The evening began very cloudy but fortunately later I was able to get a good series of observations for latitude. We had a very pleasant evening over a big fire with hot rum and water; I was very sorry for the porters who spent the night shivering over the fires round the camp — no wonder as we were about 6400′ above sea level.

16th Feb. In spite of the strong wind on top, I managed to get a sun azimuth and a round of angles which should by the sun and fix positions of Pearson's triangulations give me the position of Mening exactly. While I was doing this, Bruce built a large cairn of stone which should be visible for a long distance. We started down about 11 and reached Madial post about 1.45 pm. In the evening I had a talk with Tufnell about the whole affair of the boundary and finally persuaded him that it is no use for him to stay hanging about while we are away to the east. My object is to avoid being tied down to a day to meet him at Morongole. He can do no good now in the investigation of the frontier to the east of Madial and being fed up to tears after his 20 months of this country, thinks of nothing but getting on leave, so that he handicaps me very much in any exploration work. We agreed to make out our conclusions as to the boundary after which he will go off to Patelle and on leave. I confess I am glad to get rid of him as he has been very little helpful all through and has left all the burden of gaining information to me. I am moreover not at all an admirer of the methods of which he is the chief exponent, of dealing with the natives.

4

Expedition to Morongole and Dabosa Country
February 17th–March 14th

In this circuitous route Kelly and a large party head eastwards towards Morongole in the vicinity of the proposed boundary, and north towards Dabosa country. They cover 300 miles in 25 days. The aim of the trip was less to do with the boundary than fact-finding, particularly in respect of the tribes and tribal areas which would fall to Sudan. In spite of great difficulties with guides and interpreters, Kelly was pleased with the results. Scarcely any reference is made to the boundary, but details of tribes are recorded, together with notes about water supply and terrain. Few of the place-names mentioned in this section can be identified on maps, so the expedition's route cannot be traced with any certainty. It seems likely that Kelly put down local tribal names of particular features which did not find their way on to later maps. In a report to the Governor General of Sudan, he admits that several names on existing maps had been changed by him.

17th Feb. I had a busy morning working out the final proceedings of the Commission and arranging for our trip. Very abruptly Khamis Bensalem, the Muscat Arab interpreter whom I had picked up and who I expected to be most useful to me as he knows Arabic, Swahili and Karamojo, and moreover knows the Dabosa country well — reported sick, and Powell and Owen (the M O of the Northern Patrol)[22] having thoroughly vetted him, said he was unsound and unfit to travel. Finally with Clothier's help, I got Agwak's Katib, an educated Acholi who knows Arabic and a little Acholi, the brother of Ayom the local big man who knows Acholi and a little Karamojo, and another 'Shenzi'

---

[22] The Northern Patrol was initiated by the Ugandan administration in 1910 in an attempt to extend effective control into northern Uganda in the face of inter-tribal fighting, illegal trading, and fierce resistance to government. Several strong forces of KAR troops and police were sent on extensive tours, with Tufnell as the Political Officer in overall charge. In 1912 the patrols were largely replaced by a permanent northern garrison, although punitive expeditions continued.

who knows Acholi and Karamojo well. All this gave a great deal of trouble and I was beginning to give up hope of getting hold of anybody at all efficient. I gave Bruce instructions regarding sketching at Kideppo and to Harman instructions as to collecting supplies etc.

We finally pushed off at 3 pm, Huddleston, Powell and I with 20 Camel Corps. Powell had during our absence taken the blood of all the camels and found active trypanosomes in 19 out of 47, not counting the previous deaths about 15, which probably died of the same disease. We are taking some risk in going out with infected and weak camels but there is no alternative if we are to find out anything. We went north along the edge of the hill for 3½ miles and then turned east round it.

There was a great deal of thorn at first and we began to think that we were in for a difficult march but it afterwards thinned out and we got on better. As we had a good moon, we went on till 7.30 pm and then halted for the night. We had brought with us some donkeys to carry water for the night and grain so as to husband our own supplies; these will go back tomorrow and we should be still carrying water for four or five days, rations for three weeks and forage for about 5 days. While we were settling down for the night the auxiliary guide disappeared — the blighter — so we handcuffed the other man who is more important to us, so as to prevent any chance of his going. I wrote to Harman a letter which goes back by the donkey men, which will I hope ensure his capture and punishment.

18th Feb.   We started at 5.45 am and after a short stretch of bush came into much more open ground and turning S.E. got on well. Powell and H. had several long range shots at Jackson's Hartebeest which were plentiful though very wild. A pleasant morning's march, bush mostly very thin, sandy soil and few khors. The Kideppo lies some 10 miles east of our track but it is now I believe waterless. We did 10 miles during the morning and restarted at 3.30 for another 7½ miles. Again very many hartebeest and one was eventually bagged. We also saw a giraffe and some Grant's gazelle. Most of the afternoon we traversed over open grass plain with sandy soil, an unusual combination very good going. We halted just about 7 pm as there was thorn bush ahead and the moon was overcast. We are making straight for the peak of Lomej, a range of lower hills parallel to and west of Morongole.

We crossed a number of tracks going to Dodinga and there is evidently a good deal of communication with these hills and Nyangiya (a misnomer by the way, as the name only applies to a small hill to the west of the range).

19th Feb. A camel died during the night and another was so far gone that he had to be shot soon after we started. We turned off the line we had hitherto followed and went south, as our guide Kapollon said he knew of water. We got into the best country we have seen yet, light forest with short green grass and pretty khors. As we were going along about 7 am, we heard a snort and saw two rhino about 50 yards ahead. After a little, they trotted off still snorting like hippo. I got a lucky standing shot at a bush buck which gave us meat a little more palatable than hartebeest and we all struck at steaks of the latter at breakfast. About 8, we saw another rhino in an open space. As Powell was not keen on getting one and as Huddleston's rifle is liable to misfire, I went on. I got within about 35 yards and then waited for a shot. He was standing nearly head on and I waited till I could get a shot at his shoulder ¼ head on and then fired. He fell at once and lay kicking. It took another couple of shots to finish him off.

The horns were no longer than those we got near Tarangole but were thicker at the base. Adam amused me by cutting out a rib as an ornament to his house and some of the men licked the blood from the base of the horn after it was cut off — as an unfailing antidote against any ills. We came to a large almost continuous pool in the Khor Arus which flows north to the Kideppo and has feeders both from the south of the Nyangeir range and from Lomej. We had seen two small pools earlier. All this water accounts for the quantity of game we have seen. The water must be permanent and probably extends upstream a long distance. To make assurance doubly sure, we halted here from midday to water the camels and fill the waterskins, so that we will be provided for any contingencies. Rain came on about 1 pm and continued till after we were well on the road again. We now struck eastwards towards the hills, the going at first good as we got on to quite open ground with good sandy soil.

Quite a pretty sight of ten or twelve giraffes on the move on this plain. Eventually we got into much more intersected country with unburnt grass about 3½' high but we were much helped by elephant and game paths. A good deal of game to be seen everywhere which makes the march much more interesting. Another camel had to be shot — we are gradually losing all those which have been infected by fly and we can certainly expect to be reduced to the 15 camels which started fly free — if no worse.

It is a pity that we are handicapped in this way for if we had started with fresh camels, we could have done some really useful exploration.

20th Feb.   The rain kept off last night though there was thunder to be heard. Our route led on the right of a big hill Lawala through fairly open country, mostly sandy soil and small trees but rough patches of loam soil here and there. Powell and Huddleston were after hartebeest without success and I wounded a bush pig badly and failed to find him though I am sure he must have been lying dead in the grass near. We halted after 10 miles and rains, which had been falling most of the morning, went on during the halt at intervals. We re-started at 3.30 pm and a camel had to be shot soon after. Turning round the base of Lawala, we struck a well marked path said to come from Lomakarul (otherwise Kellere Peak), where the people, called Yom, are Dodosi and are friends with the Morongole people. We found a large waterhole in the rock 18′ × 6′ × 5′ about 50′ up a small hill joining Lawala, this was nearly full of water and according to our guide is permanent. We continued along the path which was strewn here and there with the remains of goats, probably the result of raids, which made the air rather pestilential. We halted at 6.30 after 7 miles, as we were coming over a difficult looking pass which called for the full strength of the camels. We were going nearly east all day; to the S.E. were small hills but nothing of any size.

21st Feb.   The pass was easier than it looked but nevertheless gave a lot of trouble to the camels. Our great stand-by 'Dreadnought', an enormous camel that was up to carrying 5 or 600 pounds, suddenly gave in and died on the way. Luckily the camels we have been losing on the way are all those which were infected by 'fly' so we have still a certain number of sound ones to rely on. After the pass, we traversed a very pleasant valley about 1500 yards wide, short green grass with haqlij and mablak trees; it is a pity that such good country should be quite uninhabited. Later we saw a few natives with goats and a cow but in spite of all efforts and my going on with the interpreter to talk to them, they refused to come close or to give us more information than to say that if we went on we should come to their people eventually.

A very difficult short ascent after this which tried the camels to the utmost. On the other side, we came into a confused mass of small hills but we had a well marked cattle path and got on fairly well till we came to a deep khor where we halted. This was worth seeing, the solid rock being worn into very deep pot holes here and there — there must be an enormous rush of water after heavy rain. Rain came on during the midday halt but not heavily.

Restarting about 3.30, we went on for an hour meeting traces of old cultivation but seeing no people. As it was no use dragging the camels on with no definite object, I went on with the interpreter and guide to prospect. After about 20 minutes, I saw some villages and eventually got hold of a villainous looking native, wearing a chignon, adorned with finger hooks and all the other ornaments we had heard of — a fine looking specimen nevertheless, well over 6′ high. I took him back and got hold of the rest of our people and brought them on to a good open camping place with a fine view in all directions over broken ground where zeriba'd villages were to be seen crowning the heights all round.

22nd Feb. We had a very cold night but enjoyed enormously sitting over a big fire with hot rum and milk after dinner. The natives brought in plenty of milk and wood last night and a couple of sheep last night and in the morning began bringing in a few 'garrah's' of dhurra. They declared they had scarcely any — having had their 'ginga's' raided or burnt by the Dodinga — and I think this must have been true as in spite of being paid in beads, the supply was very small. I had a brainwave to use the meat of a camel which was about to die to buy grain, and this proved popular. We eventually got about 200 lbs of dhurra (mixed red and white) and 100 lbs of flour. Another camel died later on in the morning and we brought some of the meat on to barter. A Swahili speaking native, armed with a trade gun, came in and said that 'Bwana Hindi', the man who had been sent from Madial with eight loads of iron wire — which I had sent from Nimule — to buy grain, was a couple of hours away. We had sent for Musa, a chief from Tshudi-Tshudi — about 6 hours away — who had been mentioned to me by Darley and who had been summoned to Madial by Tufnell, and were told that he had left yesterday for Madial. This was annoying as he would have been a useful guide to Mogila etc for us. As water was some way off from our camp and as we wanted to secure the balance of our iron wire and any grain that may have been bought, we decided to move on after lunch. We had had numbers of people in our camp all the morning, all rather starved-looking and not at all truculent. They — who are Dodosi — are of the same stock and talk the same language as the Karamojo, Turkana, Dabosa and Ji-ei. They have been repeatedly raided by the Dodinga — who are similar to the Beir and Boya, and appear to make no effort at retaliation. They apparently left the basin near J. Morongole proper owing to these raids and have now moved eastwards, the camp where we stopped being about their westernmost village. A fine view from a knoll behind our camp, Mogila — a long range — being visible to the N.E. We descended steeply on starting and marched almost due east to enter a wide valley, draining to Kh. Lawakuj which goes to the Arus and thence to the Kideppo, with short green grass and fine trees, red sandy soil with large clearings for cultivation. We saw large numbers of small villages, all surrounded by thick stockades; the huts are all small and individual compounds are again surrounded by zeribas, so that once inside, the people should be fairly safe. I never saw a more attractive bit of country and being about 5500 feet high, would make an ideal place for a station and given transport facilities would be productive. After about 6½ miles we came to three wells about fifteen feet deep in the sandy khor and halted in a most delightful spot on its bank under large seyal trees. I sent for 'Bwana Hindi' who appeared at sunset and reports having got 20 loads of grain which is satisfactory if true. He said Musa is still at Tshudi-Tshudi so probably the messengers we sent last night never fetched up at all. The Swahili speaking man who came in this morning and whom I had wanted to act as guide, said he was afraid first of the Dabosa, who he said were very bad people, and also of the possible lack of water. I told him to try and get a pal who knew the Turkana, as I think it possible we may see some near Singote and possibly buy camels from them. I hope we may find it possible to go to Singote and Mogila — get to the front of the Dabosa and then go back to Madial, skirting the south of the Dodinga.

This tour together with a reconnaissance southwards from Boya when we go there later should give us a good idea of the country. We may look for very bad going but if our camels last out, we should be able to get through, if we can buy some forage. I am disappointed in the Dodosi who in spite of their warlike appearance, seem poor hearted people. The older men wear the flat chignon almost down to the small of the back, made out of hair into a felt like substance this is generally hung on to the head and is not part and parcel of the natural hair. The younger men also wear their hair in a chignon which is more of the fashion adopted by women 20 years ago. Nearly all wear a broken circle, made of rhino hide like a thin 'Kurbag' stuck onto the top of the head and terminated by a tuft. They have the two central incisors of the lower jaw removed. Iron wire is not common but a few men wear high and tightly fitting collars of it. The women wear skins and in some cases carry a quantity of iron wire, many coils hanging loosely round the neck. The men take quantities of snuff which is carried in a goat's horn suspended round the neck. They seem to feel the cold very much and in the evening and early morning all carry a burning faggot for warmth. Curious capes of monkey fur or even cow hide are worn by some. Few spears were to be seen, those that were carried were sheathed. Very few wrist-knives were worn.

23rd Feb. Huddleston went off early to Hidi's place and returned before breakfast with about 1200 lbs of grain and nine loads of iron wire. I spent the morning completing my map. We had crowds of natives round and bought a good deal more grain and flour with the remains of yesterday's dead camel meat. I handed over 1¾ rolls of iron wire to Hidi with instructions to buy donkeys (this should work out to about 13 donkeys, price equal to 3 rupees each!) and take them to Madial together with the spare camel saddles. I gave him a letter to Harman detailing our plans. Musa, the chief from Tshudi-Tshudi arrived about noon but proved useless as he denied all knowledge of the country we are going to, a palpable lie according to information from Darley and Tufnell.

We started at 1 pm, at first through delightful forest but the road soon became bad and passed through very broken country with deep ravines which proved very difficult for camels. After about 7 miles we came to the edge of the escarpment, a precipitous drop of nearly 2000 feet. H. and P. started improving the path down but it proved impossible to get loaded camels more than a short distance, so they had most of the load carried down a further 600 feet where we camped on a small level space. I sent the natives with us to bring all the people from Unguluaka, the village below the scarp, to carry down the loads and they arrived about 9 pm. I seldom saw a more wonderful view than that from the top. The re-entrant of the escarpment where we have to descend is itself magnificent. Looking to the N.E. and E. there is a clear view over a vast plain cut up by hills amongst which Zingote and its northern continuation which must be Mogila are prominent. One could see Lotuke, the peak at the south of Dodinga and I still think a route can be found between there and Zulia, another large hill to the S.E. of it. One could also see Kapedo, N. or N.E. of Zulia, which is near the commencement of the Dabosa country, and though from a great height, it is hard to judge distances, it should not be a big march there from Mogila. The guides which we have picked up seem to know very little but I hope we shall pick up someone better from Unguluaka's at any rate someone from the Turkana at Zingote, if we are lucky enough to see any there. We shall feel the difference tomorrow in going down to the plain after the delightful climate and surroundings on the plateau up here.

24th Feb. Lukuta returned about 9 pm with twenty or thirty men from the villages below and they brought most of the baggage down from where the camels were to our camp by moonlight, but the cold was too much for them and they disappeared before morning. The first prospecting to the front showed a fairly easy slope and path, so after taking everything by hand another hundred feet or so lower, Huddleston shidded up and began the descent loaded. We got on fairly well at first, though very slowly with men in front to make good the rough path. I had sent off Lukuta at daylight to bring back the people from the village in case they were wanted and they appeared about 10.30 and showed us what proved to be a better though still a very difficult way to the bottom which we reached about 12.30, the last camel being down at 1.15, by dint of much tree cutting and heaving up of rocks. The last part though not quite so steep was almost more difficult than the rest, as it was very rocky. The total descent was 2000 feet and looking up at it, it looked an impossible climb down for a camel.

The men as well as the camels were pretty done when we finally reached rock pools in the khor about ¾ mile up from where we reached the bottom. Two camels succumbed on the way down but these were 'fly-blown', so their demise was to be expected. The natives worked well in path clearing and we gave them a handsome present of a ring of iron wire in the afternoon. There proved to be an abundance of good water in pools higher up the khor. As the camels were so done and as we want to start from here with the camels belly-full of water, H. decided to put off watering till tomorrow which will be the fifth day from the last watering — in this cold climate they do not want much but in future, going over the plain, we shall not be so well off. Mohammed, the interpreter, gathered through Lokuta, our Swahili-speaking native, from the natives that there is water at Singote; this information is from Turkana who came in here very recently to buy grain. Apparently now that rain has fallen, the Turkana are in this direction which is a promising sign for us. As there was no competition to accompany us as guides, we had to induce two, who appeared to know all about the country, to remain with us as guides, by handcuffing them. This is a regrettable necessity but after being sold by guides deserting a few times, one becomes rather hard hearted. The boy, Kapollon, who came from Madial, was handcuffed when we halted for the first three days, after which he has behaved like a tame dog and is quite happy.

25th Feb. We all went up the khor to see the camels watered and I did some amateur gold washing or rather washing for gold, in the sand of the khor bed. I got some bright grains but my geological knowledge did not run to identifying them so I brought the results back with me. There was a little running water in the upper part and some very large rock pools; altogether a delightfully pretty gorge. We left at 1 pm after losing another camel. We marched down the rocky khor bed for some time and struck a well marked path at the end of the hills which was said by our guides to lead to Turkana escarpments.

They said they knew of water in J. Zingote and we made straight for it about N.N.E. when the path became confused. We did 12 miles before halting, the march going over a plain with sandy soil and short 'neghil' grass and low thorn bush, very small hills dotted about. We saw a number of Grant's gazelle and I made a fruitless stalk after what I imagined to be an eland. When I got near, I saw some Jackson hartebeest galloping away and I thought I must have diagnosed badly, but when I got back, H. and P. both said they saw the eland. It often happens that eland are guarded by hartebeest, in fact I have seen them in the Lado together. At first I thought these were kudu but think now they were too brown a colour to be. I got a Grant's gazelle at the halting place, badly wanted meat; unluckily it was a female, I wanted a male head as they are the most graceful gazelle heads I have seen.

26th Feb. The country became more thorny and covered with spear like cactus grass which made nasty wounds in one's legs. We made for the gap in the hills between Zingote and Kaminyurorok, a northern continuation of the former. As the hills were approached, we got to heavy loam soil covered with stones which made going slow. Very many old tracks of game and near the gap, old droppings of camels, cattle and donkeys. The lack of new tracks made us rather give up hope of water but I went on up the rocky khor some 600 yards from its mouth and came to a large rock pool with plenty of water which must be permanent. The going in the khor was so bad that it was impossible to take the camels up loaded. This does not matter, as, having seen some fresh elephant tracks this morning which denoted plentiful water, I elicited from the guides there is another large water supply under the west side of the hill further north. Lukuda, the Carabineer as we call him, now seems to be getting more intelligent and seems to know much more of the route ahead than he confessed at first. By comparing what he said with Darley's information and the notes I got from Tufnell, I think we shall find plentiful water at Kapedo (called Lolimi by Darley) two days from the water ahead of us.

Mogila appears to be a hill N.W. of here but I fancy the hill which from Mening I took to be Mogila must be Chelom; this is the one I want to fix as the boundary. The Turkana visit the water where we now are — Loketabong — and also the water ahead but this is probably their N.W. boundary which makes Chelom quite satisfactory. We went on at 4.15, at first N.W. along the front of Kaminyurorok, but after a little, the guides turned westward and finally I found that the water they were making for lies not under the end of K. but out on the plain. As they had pointed out the water in the former place this morning and as false statements might let us in badly, I had each of them given a light beating. After 4½ miles across the uneven plain which was covered with light thorn bush we halted for the night.

27th Feb. A short march of two miles brought us to the same khor on which we 'gail'd' yesterday, now flowing in a N.N.W. direction. The guides promised us Turkana wells here; but we found one waterhole 6' deep beside the khor nearly dry and another rather deeper with some water in it. A little further on, we found some clear surface water in rock in the khor bed and we halted on it, so as to water the camels and fill up girba's before going to Mogila which lies N.N.E. apparently some 20 miles away. I learn from Lukuda that the Turkana-Dabosa boundary is the khor at Kapedo; if this is so, it is most satisfactory as it will lie just about the line which I chose provisionally with Tufnell.

We left at 2.30, making for the gap between a lower hill Kangyetak and Kaminyurorok. At first we marched down the khor (Lokomoresi) and soon after starting I saw a lesser kudu in the bed which stood and looked at me for over a minute. My fool of an orderly had put my rifle in its case and took such a long time to get it out that the kudu went off much to my disgust as I wanted one badly. The head seemed like a sitatunga and the white stripes on the body were clearly marked. Our way led over thickish bush much cut up by small khors, the soil being gravelly and rocky in places. 5¾ miles brought us to the low rocky pass, near which we saw tracks of what we thought were camels and donkeys, though the men who cannot believe that camels are to be found as far away as this insisted that the former were giraffe. We saw a couple of Dabosa graves, large piles of stones here and the guides said that they were here formerly till driven out by the Turkana. I did not mention that we saw a clearly marked track not far from our starting point which was said by the guides to be the Turkana track to Lozulia. After leaving the pass, we marched across the basin formed by the back of the Kaminyurok hills and halted having done 8½ miles over very bad going. Our food supply is beginning to show weakness in some items but we have plenty of the real essentials still.

28th Feb. Through another small pass and down some 400 feet to the Nianam river. At first spear grass and bush but a belt ½ mile wide of thick bush and trees near the river which flows about East, a sandy bed 100′ wide with 5′ banks. Powell made an unsuccessful stalk after giraffe but got a Grant's gazelle which gave us some much needed meat. Huddleston saw three oryx but did not get a shot. We halted on the river bed and I offered a 50 P.T. reward to any man who finds water; though they are all rather pessimistic, I think the place looks likely. An unfortunate occurrence is that H. lost the key of the hand-cuffs which are on a wrist each of our two guides. We must now take them to Madial anyhow which I did not want to do.

The foot of Mogila is ¾ mile away and it looks a stiff climb; the position is certainly incorrect on the map and I hope I shall be able to fix it. Water was found in the river bed about 2.30 pm, within 4′ of surface, a very slow inflow but this should suffice to water the camels and fill up girbas tomorrow. I left at 4 pm to climb the hill with five soldiers, Mohammed, the 'Musketeer' and the four 'Shenzi's'; Huddleston cut the Gordian Knot that united two of them — as they thought for life — with an axe using another as an anvil. I only took a blanket and waterproof sheet and a couple of tins of meat as I had to get the theodolite up. The climb was much longer that I expected, as I had to go a long way south to avoid the precipice that lines most of the top. I did not reach my goal which was the secondary peak about 300′

lower than the main northern peak — till 6.45. Shortly before I crossed a rocky khor which contained a large supply of water in rock pools, which must be permanent. Thus both Darley's items of information about water proved correct. There was too much mist to see much on the way up but I managed to get a latitude.

1st March A fairly comfortable night on a bed of grass which seemed to get very hard towards morning. I climbed the extra 100' to the peak early, having slept below for shelter, but was much disappointed to find a thick haze everywhere. I waited till 9.15 in the hope of it clearing but as it then made no signs of improvement, I had to descend as we cannot afford another day here. As far as I could see last night, the country to the east is a level plain with little bush; we could trace the bed of the water course for a long way by the greener appearance of the bush. I learnt from the 'Musketeer' and the 'Sisters Giggle' that there is water to be had going east to Rudolf from here but could obtain no precise details except as to water being obtainable by digging at Nawiatome (= the village of elephants) a day east of Zingote; there is water in a rock pool in the latter exactly on the opposite side from Lokitabong where we were the other day.

I came down to camp in 2½ hours; the ascent and descent were not steep but were made difficult by the loose boulders which covered the whole hillside. Tracks of zebra on top but not recent; there were also signs of old huts and cultivation on the lower slopes. I was pretty tired when I got down and indulged in my first midday sleep since I left Nimule I think. The camels were all watered with some difficulty and most of the girbas filled when we left at 4 pm. We struck off due west in the direction of the E. end of J. Zulia which I now think must have been the hill I mistook when at Mening for Mogila. Very crumbly loam soil and gravel which made going heavy most of the way. I missed a splendid chance at a fine Grant's gazelle buck owing to my soldier orderly telling me there was a round in the chamber of my rifle when there was not. We delayed a little on the way to search for water holes round a small rocky hill to which game tracks led in all directions but without result. Halted having done 5½ miles. I gather that Moro Akipi (= the hill of water) on the road to Tomadur is the same as Tirano and this I think corresponds with what Tanner, the Uganda man discovered. I let the two Shenzi from Unguluaka go here with six rounds of iron wire each to say nothing of the severed handcuffs divided between them. They knew the country but either from unwillingness or from fear, gave very inaccurate information. The 'Musketeer' having shown signs of wanting to bolt has had to be tied up for the last two days; he is valuable to us, as he knows the Dabosa country, having probably been there with the Turkana to raid — hence his fear of going there now.

2nd March We had a tiring march partly over the same heavy loam and partly through dense bush, of 9½ miles to our midday halt. I am beginning now to correlate Darley's route reports and those given me by Tufnell between Morongole and Lokalyan the first Dabosa country. I am sure that we could have got across to Lake Rudolf if it had been necessary from Mogila, but I think there was nothing to be gained by it and since we have only three day's grain and have probably some very heavy work ahead still for the camels before we rejoin Harman, I decided it would not be justifiable to go. The afternoon's march in which we only covered 5½ miles was again very trying through the densest thorn bush which tore shreds off one's clothes, arms and knees. Zulia towards which we were travelling seemed to recede as we went on. A few days of rain but not enough to clear the thundery air.

3rd March Lukuda changed his mind about the position of the water after we had been going about three miles and we struck W.S.W. towards the side of the hill, reaching a large rock pool in a rocky khor after 6 miles. We decided to halt here for midday to fill up girbas, the hot weather lately has caused a heavy drain on the supply. I saw a fine kudu when I was going on ahead towards the water and Powell later on had a shot at and wounded another. There was a large clearing, evidently the site of a former village not far from the water; probably a Dabosa village vacated after Turkana raids. I am full of curiosity to see what there is behind Zulia when we get to the N.E. corner — whether or not we shall find a feasible route back to Madial south of the Dodinga hills. Our mess stores are beginning to show signs of weakness in several items and if we cannot get back within our three weeks we shall be on very short commons. Powell went out again with a couple of soldiers and found his kudu lying dead, unluckily a female; as H. also got a small pig during the halt, we are well set up for meat. I went on ahead at 2.45 to climb an outlying western spur of Zulia so as to discover if possible a route back to Madial. From the first hill I ascended I could see little so I went up another further west and could see no chance of any route south of Lotuke, but Kapolon, the guide from Madial, told me he knew of a Khor Kalinyuro north of Lotuke, with water, which would take us out on the plain of the Apart from such considerations as the advisability of getting into touch with the Dabosa, we must go to their country to buy grain. I hope to come back by the rear of the Apetoto (?) hills and reach the Kalinyuro after having got into touch. We unluckily lost nearly an hour owing to Mohammed and Lukuda with his guard whom I left on the first hill, remaining deaf to shots and shouts and not coming down when I descended to meet the rest of the party. We only did about 4½ miles during the afternoon, all through thick bush with some trees over sandy soil; marching nearly due north. Just before we halted for the night, we were attracted by the crowds of vultures on the trees to the carcass of an elephant which had been de-tusked and apparently had only been dead about six or eight hours. We halted just beyond and went back with candles to examine the carcass which perplexed us a great deal. The trunk was cut off and lying on the ground, the tail was cut off and removed; apparently the body was to be cut open for a circle of hide over the stomach was cut off. No signs of spear or shot wounds. From the removal of the tail, I surmised Abyssinians, though the Dabosa are said to hunt as far as this. The fact that no meat was removed may be accounted for by the fact that the people may have heard our shots; failing this, natives are ruled out, for they would have taken the meat. Moreover natives armed with spears would certainly have made for the hind legs and the backside. I think either a white man or Abyssinians must have killed it. We saw at our midday halt at the water, the grass beds and fires of three men, certainly not more than two days old.

4th March   We found on the sandy bed of a khor soon after we started the print of boots as well as bare feet. These were at once connected with the elephant and the grass beds which we saw at the Zulia water. We made north for a gap in low hills and after about 6 miles we turned N.N.E. and reached a large rock pool in a deep wide khor after 9½ miles. This was a curious formation, a sudden drop of 20 feet in the rock forming a deep reservoir as well as pools below; this must be permanent and must be the Kapedo water mentioned in Tufnell's notes made ***** by an Austrian who came up this way. The camels were watered here and had good grazing. I think this must be the Laura river mentioned by Brook of the East African Syndicate.[23]

---

[23] The East African Syndicate was a company formed by wealthy British entrepreneurs who bought extensive land holdings in the Kenya ('white') highlands in 1903.

PLATE 9

Camp at Tumbo's village (March 12th).
Tumbo, a very old man was carried down, pick-a-back to see us, and he and all his people enjoyed five hours stare at us.

PLATE 10

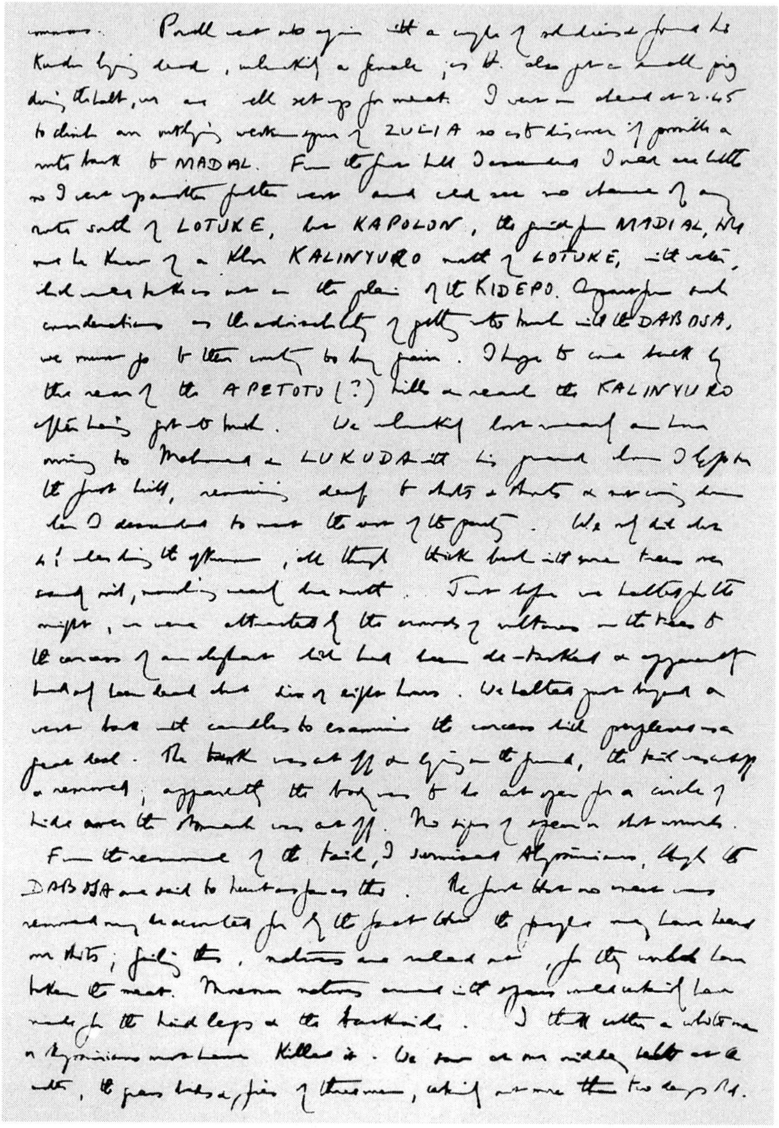

Diary entry March 3rd.

Just before we halted for the night, we were attracted by the crowds of vultures on the trees to the carcass of an elephant which had been de-tusked and apparently had only been dead about six or eight hours.

PLATE 11

Digging for water in the bed of the Kideppo (March 19th).

We crossed it just above its junction with the Kideppo and found the Sharwish and men who had been digging in the 200´ wide bed of the river to the depth of 5´ without success.

PLATE 12

Forming up after the attack on Boya (April 3rd).
Through the interpreter I told the people who were hiding there that I had burnt the other villages and taken 'dhurra', firstly because one of my soldiers had been attacked and secondly because in spite of friendly efforts, the natives had refused to bring in grain for sale.

We restarted at 4.15, turning N.N.W. and following a well marked path through undulating country with bush and covered with gravel and quartz fragments-also honeycombed quartz which I have never seen before. On the path we were very much interested to find the tracks of our booted friend and his two or three natives going and returning. We went on till dark as water was promised by the guide (in Tufnell's notes, water is placed 2 porter-hours from Kapedo) but did not reach it. The country to the west was low hills while to the N.E. and East, a wooded plain stretching to and North of Mogila.

5th March   Continuing on a well marked path, we did 8¾ miles over most uninteresting country, closely undulating, stony and covered with bush and low seyal trees. An oppressive morning with thunder in the air. I had a lucky shot and broke a young hartebeest's spine just before halting which replenished our larder at the time it was wanted. Heavy rain broke soon after the tents went up. I had my map out on the table and was overtaken by the storm which blew the tent open and soaked everything, map included. Powell came and rescued me, and held the tent up while I put the map away, much the worse for wear. It was not a little trying to have the whole of my work nearly spoilt like this, and it is the first bad mark that I have given the Camel Corps men that they pitched the tent so badly and did not come and see to it directly the storm broke. We started again at 3.30, the weather having cleared and did nearly seven miles, getting in sight [of] the hill behind which Lukuda says is the water of Lopur and Dabosa.

We passed two khors this morning with water, about 2 hours apart; near one of these were the remains of the mud houses built by a Greek elephant hunter — Moroko I think — who was in these parts some three years ago and whose camps are noted by Darley in his reports as Kampimoroko. A camel — 51 — had to be blotted out this morning, the first we have lost since Unguluaka; most of the remainder seem to be doing fairly well in spite of being on very short rations of grain. We have been marching N.W. all day and we are getting further north than I wished; we shall have a long trek back to Madial, even if we manage to find a feasible way through the Dodinga hills, and under the best circumstances we ourselves shall be very short of food by the time we get there — we have already started bread made from dhurra flour.

6th March   A pleasant evening over a large fire which was welcome again in the early morning as there was a heavy dew. We marched most of the morning over quite open grass plain, much of which being loam soil was fearfully heavy going after yesterday's rain. As the guide now says that the expected water and villages are further away than we had thought, we took it easy and only did 8½ miles during the morning. I gather that the place we are making for which the guide calls Lopur is the same as what Darley calls Kampi Moroko which is in the Zangietta. Lokalian, the biggest Dabosa centre in these parts is according to the guide near a hill visible about 12 miles north of our midday halt. This according to Darley is in the Lotileit which I take therefore to be the broad river bed by which we halted at midday.

In the afternoon we did only 3 miles — through stony undulating country with thick bush. The ridge which we saw ahead from our midday halt and which I thought must drop straight down to the Zangieta basin, proved deceptive and merely the commencement of thick broken country. We halted early as I wanted to keep clear of the Dabosa till we have plenty of daylight before us.

7th March   Clouds again prevented observations last night and light rain came on about 3.30 am. We started as usual at 6 am and after about 2 miles, Lukuda the guide became uneasy as the village he said was near, and the people 'very bad'. We got the camels together and I went ahead with Mahomed and Kapolon, as I thought it better to keep Lukuda in the background as he may have an unsavoury reputation here. I followed the sounds of cattle and men, and reached after half a mile two large cattle zeribas. I stood in the open and called to the men to come out which somewhat to my surprise they did. They appeared quite friendly and we eventually went on to the site of Morokko's huts — Kampi Moroko — near the bank of the Zanganetta about ¾ mile away, where we camped.

I sent for the headman from the village which was said to be some distance away and told the other people to bring sheep and a bull. We found they had very exalted ideas as to the value of things and refused to sell a sheep for less than 8 rounds of iron wire; bulls were not forthcoming. The chiefs arrived and I harangued them for some time through Mohamed and Lukuda, probably much of what I said was misinterpreted. I said we had come to see the boundaries between tribes so that afterwards there may be peace between them, and that perhaps next year we should send troops to settle here and see that the boundaries were observed. They said they were raided by the Boya, the Karoko (Dodinga) and the Turkana. Their boundary to the west is the Zangaiyetta while they agreed that a line between Zulia and Mogila would be quite acceptable to them. The said they had no grain and were hungry. After telling them to bring in grain and sheep, I sent them away. A pitifully small amount of dhurra and one sheep were produced, but the former we refused as the people asked such an exorbitant amount of wire for it. I was much exercised in my mind as to whether to insist on supplies as the camels have no grain and the men are running near the end of their food. I finally decided after talking the matter out with H. and P. that if we seized sheep, we should, with our small number of men, have to run the chance of having to shoot some of the people which would, even supposing the rest of the tribe in the vicinity did not collect, not be a good preliminary to peaceful occupation. It appeared to me that we shall be able to do a peaceful march through the Dabosa after we all collect together and will then without any risk of having to shoot anybody be able to shew what we wanted. I find we are within fairly easy distance of Boya with apparently no hills in the way, while if we try and make our way back to Madial via the north of Harogo, we may have to cross some very difficult country on the way without chance of getting supplies on the way I therefore decided that in view of the condition of the camels and the lack of supplies generally, it will be better to follow Darley's route to Boya and Tumbo's, which latter should be not more than 60 miles away and where we should find Harman's depôt of food. A boy whom we afterwards christened Mordkins from his habit of posturing and of wearing a strip of sheepskin around his middle like the end of a ballet dancing man's bodice, came in with a little milk for sale in the evening, and much to our surprise agreed to come with us as guide to Boya and anywhere else if his absence would not exceed a month. We zeriba'd for the night as the boy told us that the old men whom I had taken so much trouble to explain things to in the morning, had forbidden anyone to bring food and were very angry with Lukuda for bringing the 'Turks' here, so they might be making up their minds to have a go at us.

8th March We started at 6 am and soon after crossed the Zangaiyetta the boy saying he knew of *no* big river further east — the Lotilleit must be quite a minor stream. We marched nearly due west and soon got into open plain with scanty bush except dry khor beds which are lined with very thick thorn bush. The grass, only about 2′ high, was matted and mostly entangled with low thorn which soon got at one's knees. Just before halting I saw some Grant's gazelle and had three shots; I thought I had hit one but could not find it. Powell afterwards went out and the same thing happened to him. Both were afterwards retrieved, the men finding their whereabouts by the vultures over them. Mine was, I think a splendid head, over 20 inches; very unluckily the birds had already eaten part of the face and eyes away, so I can't get it mounted. Several natives appeared from nowhere and had wolfed most of P.'s gazelle before it was found. They afterwards came into the camp and said they were the scouts who were on the look-out for Dodinga raiders.

They made a long story of their wrongs as did the old men yesterday; I told them that later on we were coming to put things right but at the present moment I wanted meat and grain. They had the cheek to say they wanted some wire or beads to take back to show their people, so I told them that when the Government came to a place, it was not its place to pay a tax to the natives. They said finally they would go away and bring supplies to our night halt — a very unlikely happening. Lokolan, the khor on which we halted, has numbers of people further north — Tuliabong was on it when the Southern Column of the Beir Patrol passed through. To the south as we marched during the morning were low hills with apparently no gaps; ahead when the mist cleared a little the Boya hills were visible. We did another $5\frac{1}{2}$ miles in the afternoon. I had a long shot at an oryx, the first I have seen but unluckily missed. An unpleasant march with low thorn amongst the open grass plain, till we struck a path which was said by Mordkins to be the patrol path used by Dabosa from Lokolan who went out to keep a look-out on Boya and Dodinga raiders. I hope now we shall reach Tumbo's the day after tomorrow and get a supply of grain which we much need; all flour is finished, the men's biscuit also and we are reduced to unground dhurra whilst our own stores are down to a very low ebb, in fact altogether out in most items. We zeriba'd for the night as we are in the middle of a land of internecine warfare. We keep to the south of the main Boya hills and have apparently a clear road ahead to the Loggire hills.

9th March   A ten mile march through bush country with many small khors brought us to the N.W. corner of the separate Boya hill which forms really part of the Dodinga hills and which had been fixed by Pearson. I found I am out about $5\frac{1}{2}$ miles in longitude which I think is partly due to my original position of Mening have been fixed wrong from Harogo. This is only an error of about 2½ per cent but though this is small, I think I should be nearer than this. Unluckily there was a very thick haze all day which prevented the Boya hills being properly visible.

These are the most extraordinary jagged mass I have seen, even more fantastic in shape than the Logire hills. I shot a Jackson during the morning march and got a marabout over the carcass of a camel that had to be blotted out at the midday halt. In the afternoon we marched on a S.W. bearing, the Dodinga hills drawing back far to the left; bush country with many small khors; halted at 6.40 having done 16 miles. With luck we should be at Tumbo's if we can find it, by midday on the 11th, and should reach the Kideppo tomorrow. Two khors we crossed this afternoon should both give water by digging at an easy depth.

10th March Marched throughout the morning towards the peak of Egadung in Logire. I shot an oribi and a giraffe which was cut up and carried away almost to the last pound. He stood and watched the rest of the caravan till I got up within 150 yards in the quite open plain and gave me a good shot but he did not fall till the fourth. The skin is extraordinarily thick, I took two large pieces with the idea of making a table and stool of them. The meat was very welcome to the men, who have little else to eat now, though H. had saved up 100 lbs of dhurra for contingencies. We in the mess are reduced to dhurra flour bread which is like nothing more than fine sawdust. Ration biscuit boiled as a vegetable is excellent but we are on the last of it now. We halted at 9½ miles at the beginning of what appeared to be thick tropical forest.

We walked into the latter to see if the river Kideppo was near but after about ½ a mile of tropical vegetation, we saw no signs of it. Eventually Lukuda who by the way is now a free man, came back and reported water close to the surface in a khor. H. went down there with eight men to fill the girbas in a water hole about 3′ deep. He found some natives there who ran away at once. The tsetse fly was swarming down by the khor, even on the border of the forest they were bad. We did not start again till 4.45, plunged almost at once into the forest and after ¾ mile came to what must be the Kideppo, a sandy khor about 140′ wide with banks only 3′ high. It must overflow for some distance in the forest on either side; the trees are magnificent and the vegetation generally tropical. We dug about 4′ in the bed and came to very damp sand; there is no doubt water is obtainable anywhere in the khor at about 5′ depth at most. Crossing the river, we emerged from the forest and marched more or less along the edge till dusk. My idea is to strike onto the edge of the Logire hills and then follow south along them. By this means we should strike either Tumbo's or Suliman's village where we should get grain.

11th March   Striking in towards the hills, we met a well marked path and following up it, came to cultivation. For some little time walking along the foot of the hills in a S.E. direction, we could not get hold of anyone though we saw people in the distance but finally I induced some people to come down — Ikorro — who proved very friendly, brought down water and walked with us to show the way to Suliman's which as I thought is further along the hills. They induced us to go up a wide valley in the hills to water which they said was nearer than Suliman's. The distance proved very much longer than they led us to expect, we halted after about 11 miles, Powell and I walked on to the water another 1½ miles, a clear stream of water flowing over rock from J. Egadung, flowing into a very deep rock pool, the most grateful drink I ever had. The people proved most amenable, brought down at least thirty 'burma's' of water, about 600 rotls of grain, sheep, honey etc. P. and I were delighted to get some native tobacco which, strong as it was, was very welcome after several days deprivation. Honey in tea or cocoa is a drink which would make the fortune of a Rumpelmayer, and milk was also a very welcome addition. Suliman whom I had sent for came in to see me and I told him to prepare for us when we go on to his village tomorrow morning. He says there is no fly further down the Kideppo, so our way to Boya is evidently to keep along these hills as long as possible and march through the valley of the Kideppo at night. I sent a message to Harman to give him our whereabouts and asking him to send out some jam, bread, sugar and other luxuries for us. Our only cereal for the last few days has been a little biscuit done as a vegetable, very excellent in its way but not sufficient to take the place of bread. The people here are Logire and the local chief says they are on good terms with the Dongatolo who live on top of the hills. There was a small post of the KAR here for some time which perhaps accounts for the excellent behaviour of the people, a very marked contrast to the Dabosa; I told Mohamed — who has been most useful to us all through as interpreter in Swahili and Acholi — to give a lecture to the Dabosan boy on the subject and to let him see that everything was paid for; I fear this object lesson will be wasted as the boy has no thoughts above wolfing meat, raw if possible. I was compelled to drag him by force off the giraffe yesterday when he was supping up the blood in pints. Two more camels died last night, they have been very hungry lately, no grain for several days, and they wanted their drink today badly after 4 days without water.

12th March   We had a very short march of 4½ miles from Tumbo's which lies close under the hillside. His women brought in quantities of water from the Kideppo which lies about 2 miles away. Tumbo, a very old man was carried down, pick-a-back to see us, and he and all his people enjoyed five hours stare at us. I arranged with Suliman who is his grandson to come into Madial so that he can come out with the advance party to arrange water supply for the march to Boya. A quantity of dhurra was produced but we did not take it as we have as much as we can carry. I told Tumbo to collect all the grain he could for us to pick up on our march northwards. We started north at 3 pm and did 8½ miles along the hill striking through low passes at two places where the path was bad and rocky, and halting in a wide valley behind Sarao.

13th March   Continuing on across the valley to J. Momoi, we passed a waterhole under J. Laruwa about 9' deep which has little water at present but in which a small spring exists which could I think be enlarged so as to supply us. After Laruwa we had a cleared path to the end of Momoi where we met the road from Tarangole and the post of Kawur to Madial.

Halted a couple of miles later on Kh. Igawi in open ground. No signs of the load of luxuries which I wrote to Harman from Egadung to send out for us. We had a sharp shower during the midday halt and had an unpromising start over cotton soil afterwards but the going improved and we did 8 miles in the afternoon making 17½ during the day. I discovered after about an hour that the track we had passed before Laruwa was distinct from that which we followed and I con- cluded that our stores must have gone by it. I sent back a couple of Suliman's men to the junction of the roads with instructions to follow back along the other track if the hamla had not yet passed. About 8 pm they came back saying the soldiers and donkeys were near and bringing a letter from Harman in which he said that Bruce had been ill. We had rather expected that Bruce would come out to meet us in his usual energetic fashion and his non-appearance was thus accounted for. The stores arrived after we had turned in and we did not have the enjoyment of the luxuries they included.

14th March   The first good breakfast we had had for several days and a 7 mile march into Madial. We completed the 300th mile of this 'jolly' just before getting in — not bad going for 25 days on the road including halts, considering the country we have been over. The whole trip has turned out most successfully in spite of all our difficulties regarding guides and interpreters, and the results are far better then I had ever hoped. Huddleston deserves a great deal of credit for all he did and I never want to come across a better lot of men than his camel corps; I only wish they were going with me to Boma instead of the heavy footed men of the 12th. We reached Madial for a late breakfast and found everything going well; Bruce had had a very sharp go of malaria, having gone sick two days after we left. He had been very well looked after by Owen, the MO of the Northern Patrol.

We are well off for grain and should leave here with all we can carry. We have taken nearly the whole 18 tons which we asked Uganda to supply.

5

Interlude in Madial and Preparations for the Expeditions North to Boya and Boma

March 15th–March 17th

Kelly spends time catching up on his map, and making preparations for an excursion north to Boya, and a more ambitious expedition beyond to the Boma plateau region on the Abyssinian border.

15th, 16th and 17th March A second mail arrived besides the one we found waiting for us and I got the Amharic permit to enter Abyssinian territory which I was glad of, as it should simplify dealings with Abyssinians I may meet a great deal. After a day's rest and letter writing, I spent my time bringing my maps up to date which I nearly succeeded in doing. I was glad to find that I was only about a mile out in my map, as my position of Mening was wrongly fixed, 'Harogo' being either incorrect or it is a different point to that which I observed. This makes my whole trip from Nimule and onwards most satisfactory. Bruce seems well convalescent and will I hope be fit enough to go to Boma.

6

Reconnaissance Trip to Lotuke and Return to Madial

March 18th–March 25th

A small party, including Harman, Lilley, and an infantry escort accompany Kelly eastwards to the prominent Lotuke hill, to enable Kelly to take bearings to confirm the accuracy of his mapping. Back in Madial his mind is once more on the Boma expedition.

18th March Huddleston and Powell started for Loggire in the afternoon with a section of the 12th and the Camel Corps to prepare a water supply at Laruwa and at two points on the Kideppo on the way to Boya. H. will send in to Bruce when the Laruwa supply is available and Nushi Effendi will then go in with the main body and hamla, Bruce awaiting the return of Harman and myself.

Harman and I started at 3 pm with Lilley and a section of the 12th for Lotuke (Harogo) as I want to correct my map definitely with Zulia which is the nearest point to Lotuke which we touched on the Morongole tour. We took Ayom with us, a very unwilling guide, who had sedulously cultivated a bad eye to escape going; he is a thorough double dealer; after raiding the Dodosi with the Dodinga, he came and gave information of the presence in his house of a Dodinga chief yesterday and the latter is now in durance vile till his people produce the two men who murdered a porter on the Tereteinia road last week.

Lilley had some difficulty with his local donkeys which did not take at all kindly to our method of saddling and carrying loads. Going round the north end of the Madial range we struck out towards Lotuke, sleeping on open ground after 7 miles.

19th March 8½ miles during the morning mostly through open country; I shot a Jackson for meat just before halting. At 1.30, we sent on Ayom, Said the interpreter and six men to dig for water in the Kideppo which was said to be about 4 miles off. We started at 3.30

and after 3 miles reached a wide khor which is probably the Arus which we watered in on the way to Morongole. We crossed it just above its junction with the Kideppo and found the Shawish and men who had been digging in the 200′ wide bed of the river to the depth of 5′ without success. Said and two men had gone downstream to look for water. We still had 9 'girbas' of water so we were alright for the night anyhow and could give the donkeys a drink, so I halted here and went on digging till dark in two places without success though damp sand was found and it is no doubt that water would be found within 12 feet anywhere. Said and the two men returned about 7.30 having found water close to the surface about a mile or two away, so I sent twelve soldiers and the scally wags with girbas and water bottles to bring enough water for the night. Tomorrow we must go down to the water to give the donkeys a proper drink and fill girbas before going on. The donkeys had five girbas between them, which should keep them going.

The valley here is quite pretty, many palms and big trees, no signs of fly at present. Many recent tracks of elephant and other game. We have nearly a full moon which makes things easier. It was fortunate that we found water, as we as well as the men were pretty thirsty.

19th March The party came back from water about 10 o'clock bring-ing plenty for the night; I woke up half an hour later and heard a loud sound of chewing on all sides; the men were making up for lost time and were putting away meat at the rate of about five pounds an hour. We started at 6 am for the water and marching more or less along the right bank of the Kideppo reached the spot after 3 miles. The water was in shallow holes about 2′ deep on the side of the river at a spot where it must overflow to nearly 600 feet in the rains, the shallow sandy river bed itself being about 200′ wide. It was on the track we crossed after our midday halt yesterday going to Dodinga and must be frequently used. I gather the Bira people are actually Dodinga which accounts for the frequent communication and for the fact that they keep their cattle with the latter. We gave the donkeys their much needed full watering and filled all our 20 girbas before starting at 9.30.

We only did 4 miles towards Lotuke in a couple of hours marching mostly over open undulating country draining to the Kideppo and gradually rising. After lunch we did 6½ miles halting about 5.40 in order to make a zeriba. I shot a good Grant's gazelle shortly before the halt and took the mask for mounting. The Dodinga hills now appear an unbroken high ridge, quite unlike their appearance from Mening. There were very recent tracks of elephant on the Kideppo and the water party heard trumpeting close to them last night at the water place, but outside on the plain we saw no traces of any big game except of rhino. It seems according to Ayom that Lotuke is uninhabited and that between it and a prominent hill called Loreima (the chiefieta) there are few people. The Kideppo river, as far as one can see, rises on the north side of Morongole but there must be an important feeder ahead of our night halt coming from Lotuke. Lilley and I intend going on tomorrow morning to Lotuke, the col to the south of it appearing to be about 5 miles away, as I want to see what there is between there and Zulia on the proposed frontier line.

21st March   Lilley and I started at 5.30 with 4 soldiers and my scally-wag following of guides etc. for the south east spurs of Lotuke. The distance was very deceptive and we found it was about 7 miles to a small hill near the end of Lotuke from which I could survey the country. I found there is behind Lotuke an apparently pass-less low range, which coincides with what I gathered from my view from Zulia. Between these and the front of Morongole is a series of low hills with apparently a pass at the southern end. I see nothing for it but to carry the frontier line from the hill I was on round the south of the spur of Lotuke and then direct to the Northwest end of Zulia. All this country is uninhabited, even the north western slopes of Morongole are so, and the frontier is so far satisfactory. Lotuke was formerly inhabited but owing to Dodosi retaliation, the people went further north. North of Lotuke is a practically continuous high ridge extending north, sparsely inhabited as far as Loreima where the bulk of the Dodinga live. I am uncertain whether or not the Dodinga and Karokko are one or whether they are natives of the same tribes. According to Said, the interpreter from Madial, the northern Dodinga and Dabosa are friendly. These may be the true Dodinga, the southern people, enemies of the Dabosa whom we met may be Karokko as distinct from Dodinga.

We saw a rhino on the march out but did not disturb him as I had no time to spare. I got back to camp before ten o'clock, having done 14 miles, climbed a hill and taken a round of bearings in 3½ hours. The message I sent on to Harman by Lukuda, telling him to start, only reached him five minutes before I arrived, so we all moved off together back towards the Kideppo about 10.15. Retracing our steps, we halted about 12, having done 6 miles. Ayom failed to turn up and we had to send back two soldiers along the road to look for him. The hamla was attacked by a rhino — at a safe distance — being the morning; the Shawish had a shot at him and *says* he wounded him. We had none too much water and were all pretty thirsty, the donkeys getting 5 girbas between them and all the men four between them, one having been pierced by thorns — by careless driving. We re-started about 3.30 and reached the Kideppo water about 5.15. It was a great luxury to get a shave and bath, the first bath of any kind since leaving Madial. Ayom arrived about 6 pm, saying he had lost his way, not being able to see on account of his bad eyes. He had planned this excuse for not going with us but having been bandaged up by Powell, tore off the bandage two hours after leaving. I gave him a lecture this morning which I told him to pass on to the Dodinga regarding the retaliation which would overtake them from both Governments if they continue in their present evil raiding practices. Everyone was very happy and contented in the evening-except probably the two soldiers who went back to look for Ayom and did not come in till 8 pm.

22nd March Starting with our twenty girbas full, we followed the path, used apparently by the Birra people who come down here to hunt and make the watering place their centre — till we reached the spot we 'gail'd' upon our way out. The path here made for a part of Nyangiya further south than we wanted to go, so we struck across country towards the villages N.W. of Mening. The distance proved deceptive and finding the villages further than I thought, I halted after 9 miles and sent Said on to tell the people to bring down water. The Birra people here were driven down from the hill top and made to settle at the foot by Tufnell[24] — in my opinion a most arbitrary and unnecessary proceeding. We went on at 3.30 having collected some water and did 5 miles through the thick bush along the hill keeping a couple of miles from the foot. We had enough water to give the donkeys a drink and even to have a small wash ourselves besides giving the men plenty. I am very glad I managed to do this trip across the Kideppo valley, as it gave me a much clearer idea of the lie of the country and the formation of the Dodinga hills which are not a collection of separate hills as I thought but a solid continuous range.

[24] The resettlement of Birra villagers by Tufnell mentioned here was presumably on a former occasion with the Northern Patrol.

23rd March   We had an easy 6 miles march into Madial. Huddleston had written in to say he had opened out the Laruwa supply and that there was enough to water all the donkeys. Nushi Effendi had therefore left the day before yesterday with the transport and remainder of escort.

Bruce and I commenced sorting out our stores for Boma; I found I have about 7 boxes of spare stores allowing for enough to last us till the end of July. Harman was down with fever in the evening and Owen rather alarmed me by saying he thought he might be in for a long go of malaria as Bruce had. If this had proved to be the case, I should have had to go and leave him here.

24th March   Owen took Harman's blood and I am glad to say found him free of malaria. Harman was not fit to march so I wrote to Powell at Aganamoi to say we would leave tomorrow instead of today. I spent most of the day plotting out my map and the route to Lotuke which worked out satisfactorily. I gave Lilley a tracing to send in to the Chief Secretary, showing the position of Lotuke, Zulia and Mogila. The mistake which Tufnell and I made in thinking the hill which is actually Zulia was Mogila, is immaterial as the line from the south of Lotuke to north of Mogila actually passes immediately to the north of Zulia.

25th March   Wilkinson, who is now acting D.C. at Madial very kindly gave me an 'askari' Mohammed Said to act as Arabic-Swahili interpreter for the Boma trip. I have also Lukuda as Swahili-Kara-mojo interpreter, though at the last moment he said he wanted to go back to Dodosi. Lokitari claims Mordkin seems homesick and afraid that he will never get back to his native land; this disappoints my hopes that he will stay with us, learn civilisation and come out again as interpreter later. We left at 3 pm and did 7½ miles during the afternoon.

7

Expedition North through Dabosa Country towards Boya and Boma

March 26th–April 12th

This large expedition to the north appears to have had two objectives. First, to allow Kelly to evaluate the prospects for Sudanese adminis- tration of the region, especially regarding the attitude of the tribes. Secondly, to press much further north east into the Boma plateau region with a view to ascertaining Abyssinian influence there. The diary ends on April 12th with a sad note about a Court of Enquiry convened to consider the death of a Sudanese soldier. Reports written by Kelly to the Governor General, however, take the story of the expedition to April 25th. On that day Kelly and Huddleston set out for Boma with an escort of 29 camel corps and 10 other men, along with 48 camels, mules, and donkeys, while the rest of the force proceeds to Boya. There is great concern throughout about access to water and provisions for men and animals, largely because of the hostility of the Dabosa tribe. Kelly's attempts to establish friendly relations with the Dabosa were largely unsuccessful, and he concluded that they wanted neither peace nor government 'nor any other strangers in their country'. Near Boya, Kelly felt obliged to adopt punitive measures both in response to attacks on his troops, and to procure much-needed grain. Several villages were burnt, and supplies of dhurra were seized. The record of these days, together with Kelly's commentary, provide valuable insights into the respective attitudes of the indigenous people, and of Kelly as representa- tive of their would-be colonial overlords. Harry Kelly emerges as a brave and dedicated man with considerable determination, whose view of the native people seemed more enlightened than that of many of his contemporaries. At the same time he used strong-arm tactics where these appeared necessary.

26th March   We started at 3 am, marched 10½ miles in fair moonlight and reached the gap at the S. end of Mommoi where we had breakfast.

Going on at 8.30 we marched 5½ miles into Laruwa where I got a letter from Huddleston saying Nushi Effendi had arrived at Aganamoi having only been able to water about 20 donkeys at Laruwa owing to the water supply running out. The two soldiers left at Laruwa said Nushi arrived there at 10 am and left at midnight having filled about 30 girbas for the 13 mile march to Aganamoi. They also said that they themselves had after Nushi's exploration removed a stone and mud that was blocking up the spring. This is rather typical of an Egyptian officer — lack of resource and sense of proportion. Huddleston also wrote to say he was leaving

Aganamoi's for the Kideppo on the afternoon of the 23rd — Suliman had failed to turn up to guide him — possibly fearing to go to Boma.

We went on at 4.30 pm for 4 miles. The people at Laruwa said that the soldiers at the post near Aganamoi treated them badly when there was no white officer present. This system of detached posts without a British officer is very liable to abuse and I must confess there is little to choose between the much condemned Belgian system and that pursued here, if the complaints made have any foundation in fact. I told the chief he should go in to Madial to complain to the Commandant if he had any cause. I think I have the sorest feet in Africa, caused by wearing ammunition boots to which I am reduced, having absolutely worn out my other boots in the last 'jolly'.

27th March   A very rough march of 10 miles to the camp where we found the main body of the escort under Nushi Effendi with the hamla at Aganamoi's, about 600 yards west of the spot we camped with the camel corps on our return from Dabosa. We stopped a few minutes at Tumbo's on the way, the old man — more like the old Duke of Cambridge than ever — wrapped in his old red blanket, said Suliman his grandson had gone to Boya with Huddleston. I was glad to learn this as H. had written to say S. had failed to turn up. We had a quiet day in the really pretty valley with the jagged mountains all round. I made a large present of stores to the Egyptian officers' mess, as I have far more than I want. Huddleston wrote to say he had opened up the water at the previous water holes on the Kideppo and had failed to find water at a suitable distance in advance of this in spite of digging to 10 feet. He had finally stopped at water he had found about 5 miles north of the first watering place. I wrote to him telling him to go on to Boya to prepare water supply there if Suliman thinks it will not

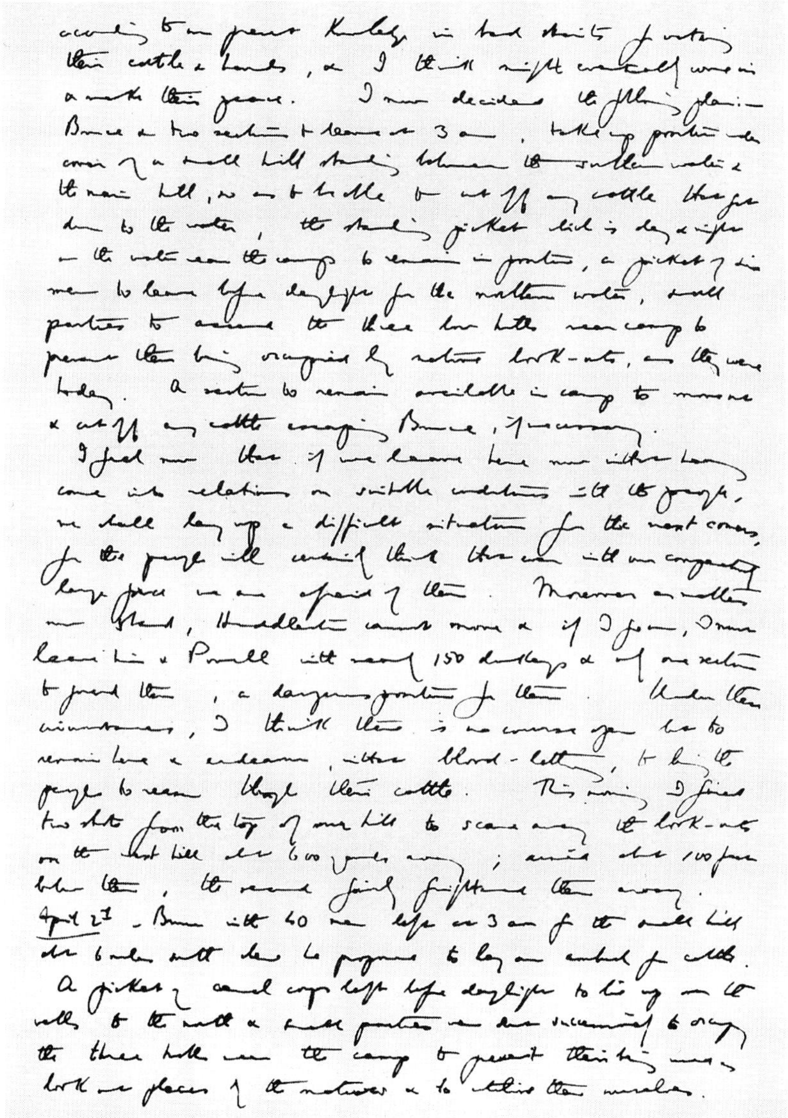

PLATE 13

Diary entry April 1st–2nd.

Moreover as matters now stand, Huddleston cannot move and if I go on, I must leave him and Powell with nearly 150 donkeys and only one section to guard them, a dangerous position for them.

PLATE 14

The 'intelligence staff': Adam, 'Tweedle Dee', 'Charles 1'. Kelly's servant Adam 'had the task of pushing the perambulator wheel, which he did not enjoy.'

PLATE 15

Toposa (or Dabosa) guides (probably April 9th).
The son of the chief from the midday halt and his three friends stay with us, the former says he was with Darley when he came to Loggire and seems an intelligent and well meaning youth.
The chief's son may be the young man on the left.

PLATE 16

Watering mules on the march from rainpools. Finding adequate water for men and animals was a constant cause for concern.

otherwise suffice. I also told him my proposed timetable of marching. The chief here was absent with the KAR detachment and we consequently found difficulty in getting anything done in the way of supplies or of work on the road, but a fatigue party worked all the afternoon in clearing the road through the bush for the rest thus three miles so that we can get on allright at an early hour tomorrow.

28th March   We started at 4.30 am, delayed a little by the disappearance of Lukuda and Lokitari. Some men were left behind to look for them. We followed the track along the foot of the hills for about 5 miles and then struck out onto the plain, open for the most part, and halted at 8.30 having done 10 miles. The two missing ones were brought in by the men left behind who had caught Lukuda early — handicapped by his self-inflicted wound in the foot — and had then been clever enough to offer beads to the natives for the capture of Lokitari. It seems that Lukuda had persuaded the boy to run away and go with him to Dabosi; he had cut a wound in his foot for which I sent him last night to the doctor and had hoped to be left behind in consequence.

The boy had my camera slung on him and had left it hung up in the Egyptian officers' grass hut. I awarded Lukuda 12 lashes for being the chief culprit and the boy 6, but gave the latter the very real punishment of taking away the clothes I had given him. It was a curious psychological fact that the four days during which he had covered his nakedness had made him very conscious of the latter. The development of this boy has been one of the most interesting things I have come in contact with for a long time — his gradual appreciation of his nakedness after a few days close contact with clothed people, the anxiety which he then displayed to cover it, his efforts at making himself useful and the really intelligent way in which he had picked up the manipulation of my perambulator wheel, the shidding of a saddle and the loading of the donkeys. If it had not been for the bad influence of Lukuda who is a thoroughly bad type in every way, he would have turned out well. As it is, I will give him back his clothes in a couple of days and have still hopes that he may turn out well.

In the afternoon we marched 5 miles mostly over open country and halted about 1000 yards away from the Kideppo which here is a khor of about 100 feet wide and on the west bank has only a 100 yards belt of trees. The advance party we had sent on two hours in advance had opened 14 water holes, water being within a foot of the surface. This party spent the night on the water with fires to keep the animals off and the donkeys will be watered at 4 am tomorrow. Even when we got in at 6 pm, there were still a few fly. I got a letter from Huddleston by Pig-Eye to say he had gone on to Boya with Powell leaving our NCO and 2 men at the water 5 miles downstream of where we now are. He says that a few fly have now appeared at the latter place and we must therefore cross elsewhere.

29th March   Harman started watering at 3 am and we left camp at 6 — keeping about ½ mile outside the belt of forest. Huddleston had told me the next water was about 4½ miles north, so I began to look about after 5 miles to see the NCO and 2 men who had been left to guide us. After I had fired two shots, they came running out, having kept a very poor look out apparently. I halted about 1000 yards away from the water and arranged that a large party should go down together to fill up girbas so that fly might not be brought up by people straggling up and down from the water. I saw a couple of fly at our camp but no more were seen. Harman went out with a party to clear a path through the forest about ¾ mile north of the watering place where we might escape fly. Very heavy rain came about 2 pm, so that we had to postpone departure till 4 pm instead of starting at 3. We crossed the khor after ½ a mile, very many deleib palms on either side; the Kideppo here was only 100′ wide with 3′ banks and sandy bed; it takes a bend to the west here. Leaving the forest belt which is quite narrow we emerged on open cotton soil country with scattered thorn bush. Luckily the ground had been so dry before that after the short interval, it had quite dried up again. Had it not been so, we would have had a bad march as the cotton soil was very heavy. We were fortunate in finding a sandy patch to camp on, as more rain threatened. I gave Lokitari back his clothes today much to his joy, it was a bitter blow to him to have them taken away. His semi-taming reminded me very much of the story of White Fang by Jack London which I read the other day.

30th March   We moved off at 4.15 and marching towards the separate N.W. hill of Boya over open country with thorn bush patches, halted after 7¼ miles to rest the animals and breakfast. We found a certain amount of water here in a rock hole in a small hill and this we covered in with thorn bush to serve for the return journey of the escort to Tarangole. Many tracks of cattle but no signs of people. Nearing the hills we saw some men sitting on the top of one who signalled as we got abreast of them. These proved to be some of Huddleston's party showing us the way to the water which was not in the position I thought, i.e. the point where the southern column of the Beir Patrol[25] met the khor. H. and his party had arrived here yesterday afternoon and found wells in the khor guided by Suliman (who had come here as a hired assassin with a party of Swahili and Baluchis[26] to avenge the murder of some of their fraternity by the Boya people). They had also come to wells about 6 miles further up the Khor Boya. They had approached the nearest villages to the camp, but distant about 2 miles, and a number of people came down the hill to meet them. H. and Powell accompanied by Suliman and Mahomed the interpreter went to the foot of the hill, and after some parleying, it appears that things began to look uncomfortable as the people would have none of them. During the afternoon there were a number of people round the camp who asked for presents of iron wire and were altogether insolent. Numbers of cattle were brought down to water. They refused to bring dhurra or anything else.

At 3 pm I started with Powell and a section of the 12th to investigate the khor to the north and try and get in touch with the people of the N.W. hill. Following down the khor — a sandy bed about 60′ wide with many large trees-we found a number of wells about 4′ deep with good water. We saw a few cattle being driven about leisurely but could get no-one to come and talk to us. The khor suddenly at a point due west of the hill degenerated into a 5′ wide channel through cotton soil and making a wide detour to the north and then west we found the khor absolutely disappeared spilling itself into a dry marsh — a most peculiar physical characteristic which must be common to the Kideppo, Zangaiyetta and the other rivers which feed the Pibor.

On the way back we approached the N.W. hill and called to the people whom we saw on top to come down, speaking through Mahomed and Lukuda (Charles I). It seems that Dabosan is the language of the people and not the Dodinga language, though some of the people knew the latter and a few also the Lango talk. A few men with spears and shields came near the bottom of the hill but would not be induced to approach nearer though I went out to meet them with the interpreters. At first they said they would come tomorrow; I explained

[25] The Beir Patrol was one of a number of punitive expeditions mounted by the Sudan government against rebellious tribes. Captain Kelly was on the patrol which subjugated the Beir between January and April 1912. (See M. W. Daly, *Empire on the Nile* (1986), 148–149).
[26] The reference to 'Baluchis' is puzzling. The word is not easy to read, but it apparently reads 'Baluchis' (people whose homeland is in Iran).

we were the same people who came here last year and camped on the khor (i.e. as the Beir Patrol) but this did not seem to impress them at all. Finally they said to Lukuda 'Why have you brought the Commandant here, we don't want him or anything to do with him'.

Returning to the camp, I found Suliman who had returned from the mission on which I had sent him — to tell the elders to come in and talk to me; he talked to the people who were hanging about the watering place and they would have nothing to do with him and refused to come in. My position was not an easy one — we want dhurra badly, having only a couple of days supply for camels and mules (owing to mis-statements on the part of the Supplies Officer Mustafa Effendi), we have the force to deal with any contingency and had the villages been on the flat and had we been able to surround them without loss to either side, we could have taken what we wanted and left full payment for it. As it is, the villages are built on the hill side and it is improbable that we could have got into them without loss. I came to the decision that we must make a reconnaissance tomorrow of the villages first seen by H. and decide definitely whether one of them could be taken without the likelihood of loss. Bruce however who had been watching from the top of a hill the manoeuvres of the people of the hill I had approached, proposed a better scheme. He said that on my approach, all the cattle had been driven into the bush in two directions and he suggested that if we caught some cattle we could hold them till dhurra was produced whereupon we would make payment. This scheme I decided to try as being the only one which offered a chance of getting what we want without risking loss to us or necessitating shooting any of the natives.

I am now unable to do what I wanted that is to leave a depot of stores and donkeys here under Mustafa Eff. with a section. It would have been an anxious job for anyone, let alone a very incompetent Egyptian. I can see no other way than to send them to Tarangole where Mustafa can collect supplies for the return journey of the escort. It is impossible to go through the Dabosa country encumbered with a transport of 300 donkeys.

31st March   We all climbed the big rock hill near the camp after breakfast to survey the country and make a 'tartib'. There were numerous villages to be seen on the hillsides, clearly arranged apparently so as to cover each other. Numbers of cattle and sheep were to be seen at the foot of the hills to the east, some 3 miles away, and they appeared to be being driven off towards the water in the khor some 5 miles south but we could not see their further course. Two men were left on the look out on top to give news when any cattle appeared near. Just as we were sitting down to lunch they came down to say cattle were being driven down from the hill to which I went yesterday towards the water downstream of here. Harman took out the two sections which had been waiting under arms all the morning; Powell and I also went out to see what was happening. We got out to the small hill near which the Southern Column Beir Patrol camped and Harman climbing this said he saw the tail end of a herd disappearing to the north a long distance away. It was useless to follow them up with heavy footed infantry so leaving Bilel Eff. with a section ambushed under the hill and a couple of men on look out on top out of sight, the remainder were marched back to camp extended as much as possible in full view of the hill where this village is in order to lead them to believe we had all returned — I fear this little stratagem was too flimsy to take in the scouts who watch all our movements. During our absence the hamla animals had been driven in for safety's sake. Huddleston was down at the water holding two natives in conversation till my return. Bruce went down to hear what they had to say and after a long interval sent back to me to say they reported having no dhurra and that they were not a little suspicious. I went down and was just telling them through Lukuda that I did not wish to discuss matters with two young men but that if the old men came in I would talk to them — when an old man came down carrying a small cow elephant tusk as an offering. When he came near, he put his spear on the ground and stepped across it twice, taking up dust at the same time and making the motion of spitting on it and throwing it towards me — all this a sign of peace. I gave him a big talk but he said they had no dhurra, it all having been attacked by birds, weevils etc.

Finally, I said I would take him up to the camp and give him a present in exchange for the tusk. He was all for running away at once but Bruce was too quick for him. The moment one of the soldiers stepped towards the old man, the other two disappeared like lightning, doubtless to spread the news we were killing the old man. Bruce led the old man up to the camp by the arm, giving him consoling talk the while. When he saw the zeriba, he made a desperate effort to get away and when that failed, he seized handfuls of dust and swallowed it — in token of absolute submission and made the motion of staggering in under repeated loads of grain. He was brought up to my tent and samples of all our trade goods were laid in front of him; as each bag was opened, he gave vent to more and more extravagant expressions of joy and surprise, doubtless a little exaggerated in order to please! Finally he was sent off with a present of various kinds of wire and beads and told to bring in quantities of grain etc early tomorrow. I should not be prepared to bet very heavily in favour of it coming! Bilel Eff. drew a blank and returned empty handed.

Mahomed the interpreter now says he wants to come along with me, rather an embarrassment of riches in the way of interpreters! Powell's syce, a soldier, found his mules missing and went out at 6.30 to look for them, three men were sent out to look for him without success. Bruce sent up some rockets.

April 1st No signs of the syce, men sent out in different directions reported his tracks going towards the small hill where we breakfasted on the 30th. Huddleston down with a severe go of fever, Powell rather perturbed at his condition as he could keep nothing down and was inclined to collapse. Cattle reported going south by our look out on the hill and I decided to kill two birds with one stone and send out a couple of sections under Bruce to look for the missing man and also to picket the wells in the khor about 5 miles to the south. They started off at 11 am but a quarter of an hour later the missing syce turned up having been to the breakfast hill after the mules which he thought might have gone back there and slept in the 'ghaba'; he saw several 'abied' but was not molested. The officious signallers signalled to the hill 'Retire' which was sent on by the signaller there to Bruce and he returned in consequence. He re-started at noon, and news was soon afterwards brought in that cattle were seen between here and the main hill, and the camel corps section were sent after them. Harman and I went up the hill to see what was going on. We could see many herds returning from the direction of the southern water, driven fast. Later we saw cattle coming down from the northern hill and Harman went down to collect a party and go after them. I stayed up on the hill till 2.30, could see cattle and goats in numbers near the foot of the main hills. The lot that Harman was after disappeared entirely. The camel corps returned with a capture of six goats only. Harman also returned with no success, cattle had been watering at the northern wells, but he could see no signs otherwise. Heavy rain came on about 3.30, Bruce came in soon afterwards. He had not been down as far as the wells but had rounded up 23 calves and 275 goats.

He had seen numbers of natives who had run away. Before he came back, I had made up my mind to send out kits and food to his party and let them stay on the water till tomorrow. With that water, the water near our camp and that to the north all picketted, the natives would be — according to our present knowledge — in bad straits for watering their cattle and lands, and I think might eventually come in and make their peace. I now decided the following plan: Bruce and two sections to leave at 3 am, take up positions under cover of a small hill standing between the southern water and the main hill, so as to be able to cut off any cattle that get down to the water, the standing picket which is day and night on the water near the camp to remain in position, a picket of six men to leave before daylight for the northern water, small parties to ascend the three low hills near camp to prevent them being occupied by native look-outs, as they were today. A section to remain available in camp to move out and cut off any cattle escaping Bruce, if necessary.

I feel now that if we leave here without having come into relations on suitable conditions with the people, we shall lay up a difficult situation for the next comers, for the people will certainly think that even with our comparatively large force we are afraid of them. Moreover as matters now stand, Huddleston cannot move and if I go on, I must leave him and Powell with nearly 150 donkeys and only one section to guard them, a dangerous position for them. Under these circumstances, I think there is no course open but to remain here and endeavour, without blood-letting, to bring the people to reason through their cattle. This morning I fired two shots from the top of our hill to scare away the look-outs on the next hill about 600 yards away; aimed about 100 feet below them, the second fairly frightened them away.

April 2nd Bruce with 40 men left at 3 am for the small hill about 6 miles south where he proposed to lay an ambush for cattle. A picket of camel corps left before daylight to lie up over the wells to the north and small parties were sent successively to occupy the three hills near the camp to prevent their being used as look-out places by the natives and to utilise them ourselves. I went up our 'signal' hill after breakfast but came down after ½ an hour, having seen no signs of cattle, as a signal message reported that the ombashi sent to the furthest of the three hills had been wounded. I met Harman filling in wells in the khor below signal hill and we went on to the hill where the affray occurred. We found it a really difficult climb of smooth bare rock and had to go barefoot. I made up my mind that we have now no alternative but to attack some of the villages, take away dhurra and burn the huts, with as little bloodletting as possible. My reasons were these: — we have tried both with a small advance party and when the main body arrived to get into friendly relations, we have shewed trade goods and given some to our elderly visitor, and now they have shewed that they intend to attack isolated parties; any party that comes after us, small or large, will be met in a hostile manner or not met at all; sooner or later stern measures will have to be taken and if the people see that with as large a force as ours, we are afraid — this would be their natural interpretation of our attitude — to attack them, we shall have done far more harm than good and shall have made them despise the Government entirely. Harman and I made our plan of attack from the point of vantage on the hills, and then returned down the really rather perilous rock face, which we neither of us enjoyed at all. When we got back to camp, I interviewed the wounded onbashi whose story was almost exactly the same as that of the soldier who was with him.

Three men had started for the hill, one man for some unexplained reason could not climb up it, so the onbashi and one man went up. Arrived on the top the onbashi left his man to watch and then went down the other side a short way. He says he turned round to look in another direction, heard a noise and found a native about to spear him. He attempted to load but the man stabbed at him and closed at once. He was stabbed in the hand by one spear and got some very nasty cuts by gripping the blade of the other. They rolled on the ground together and seeing some other natives just below coming back, he called to his comrade who ran up. The onbashi rolled out of the way and the other man shot his assailant, who was wounded but got up and was shot again, this time apparently dead, but though Morgan the man who fired the shots says his friends came and carried him away dead, the onbashi could say nothing on this point, and as we saw copious blood in the track said to have been followed, it is more likely that the man was only wounded. Bruce came back about 2.30 pm having seen no cattle or herds at all. His ambush had succeeded admirably; he had arrived at his hill by daylight and had remained hidden there with his 40 men for five hours during most of which time the natives had a lookout on the top of the very hill. Bruce says the cattle must all have been driven off to the south, possibly to the north of the Dodinga range, but I am inclined to think that after yesterday's heavy rain, there must have been water enough near the hill without going further afield to water their cattle. There was plenty of surface water in the khor where it ran through cotton soil.

Harman went out with some men in the afternoon and cleared a path through the thick thorn bush as far as 'Centre Hill', about 1½ miles; between there and the villages we are going for — a distance of 2 miles — the ground seems more open.

April 3rd We were a little late at getting off — about 4.15 am — but the start was made in silence, no fires or candles lit. Signallers were dropped at 'Centre Hill' and we reached the edge of the clearing which extends along the foot of the main hills, at about 1000′ distance, a little before 6. Till we emerged from the bush, there was absolutely no signs of life anywhere but when we shewed ourselves, we began to see cattle and goats being driven up the hill. Bruce with two sections attacked the left hand village from the left flank. One section remained in reserve about 300′ from the foot of the hill, chiefly to keep a watch for any hostile movements above the attacking party. The camel corps section was on the right ready if necessary to seize cattle etc. driven down from the hill or to stop any hostile movements from the right flank. The plan succeeded entirely and would, I think, have done so even if there had been considerable opposition, for it would have been possible to cover with rifle fire from below the attack throughout. The first village taken without any opposition or signs of people, Bruce moved along the ridge to the right and occupied the villages there successively. No signs of dhurra to be seen in any of the villages, which were then burnt. Bruce rounded up a herd of about 400 sheep and goats and a few cattle, and they were driven down to the reserve section. Meantime we discovered a cave behind the first village with a number of 'burmas' full of dhurra and other baggage. This led to a thorough search and altogether 5 'caches' were found. A helio message was sent to Centre Hill and thence by flag to camp, asking for 60 donkeys to be sent with sacks and these arrived about 11 am. All the time natives were to be seen on the hills and they, according to Lukuda, were hurling abuse at us and threatening immediate attack. The nearest approach to an attack was a rock being hurled down from the top of the hill on which we were collecting dhurra; splinters from this hit Harman. The four men who were on the top were, simultaneously with the rock hurling, spotted by the camel corps picket who fired on and killed one man.

Very strict orders were given by me, both in written orders of yesterday evening, and during the operation, that unless the natives made actual signs of attack, fire should be directed to frighten and not to kill, and that on no account was any indiscriminate firing to take place which might hit women and children in a village. In order to impress the people with the power and range of the rifle, we, the British officers, fired a good many shots near men who were just to be seen with glasses. A great deal of delay was caused by the onbashi who had in the morning found a 'cache' of grain near the furthest village we took on, being unable to find it again in the afternoon.

In all we got something over 5000 lbs of grain, mostly dukhm, though there was also red and white dhurra and telabun. The camel corps worked awfully well both in carrying the grain down the hill and in keeping a look out from prominent peaks so that the grain collectors might not be inconveniently disturbed. I imagine the grain must all have been removed from the villages during the last few days, the 'caches' were all in rock caves, the grain being either heaped up on ox-hides or in large 'burmas' (which had handles like the Beirs have). We got several curios in the caves. I got a bead helmet very similar to the Beir kind; a number of beautifully shaped wooden spoons were found, a few very wide wrist-knives (a circular plate about 9 inches diameter, sharpened all round but with the edge protected by a thin narrow leather band), several shields were amongst the things found. I let the flock of goats go, with the idea that the natives should see we had asked for grain and being refused, had taken it and nothing else. I was undecided as to returning the loot of curios too, but thought this would be rather quixotic under the circumstances.

We did not finally get away from the hills till about 5.45, much later than I wished. I went off with the interpreters to the foot of the hill further north, where a big village, the nearest to those we burnt, was situated. Through the interpreter I told the people who were hiding there that I had burnt the other villages and taken dhurra, firstly because one of my soldiers had been attacked and secondly because in spite of friendly efforts, the natives had refused to bring in grain for sale. I said that now, if they came in to make their peace they would be well received. They answered apparently in a very insulting strain to the effect that they did not want peace and would have nothing to do with the Government. I said that I had left the cattle and goats which we had taken to show that we only took what we first asked for. They finally shouted after me, as I left, that the reason I had left the goats was that I was afraid they would come and take them away from me. Matters are still in an impasse, as I fear there is no chance of their coming in unless we sat down here for weeks.

There is evidently no way of dealing with these hill peoples except the continued exhibition of force — the Uganda methods, though much more drastic than those we employed today, are I fear the only effective ones. As far as we know for certain, only two natives were killed today — one of whom was one of the party rolling stones down — and I sincerely hope there were no other casualties. The day's work entirely corresponded to my programme, and it was most fortunate that we had no casualties at all. We got back to camp about 6.45 pm and I am glad to say found Huddleston up and much better. Powell thinks he will be ready to go on with us in a couple of days; the most serious ailment had been blood poisoning of the foot which P. thinks may have been chiefly responsible for the fever. The man with the wounded hand is getting on fairly well but may be deprived of the use of some of his fingers.

4th April Very heavy rain during the night which reduced the camp to a quagmire. I gave orders that any natives seen should be encouraged to come in — a very far remote contingency I am afraid. If nothing else happens, I now intend sending Mustafa Effendi with a section and spare donkeys to Tarangole tomorrow to buy food for the escort's return journey; another section will accompany them till they are out of harm's way. Rain again during the morning.

In the evening Harman and I went up the hill to point out the route to Tarangole to Mustafa Eff. and to Nushi Eff. the Yuzbashi who accompanied him for the first march out. I decided to send them straight from here to the gap between Ilio and Chalamini, a distance of about 25 miles. Probably they will find water on the way after this heavy rain and in any case they will get water at Ilio where Suliman says the people will bring it down from the hill.

5th April Rain again during the night. Preparations during the morning for the party leaving here this afternoon. I wrote a report to the Sirdar re the episode here and also reported it to the OC Madial. I am sending the Uganda soldier back to Madial as I have agreed to take Mahomed on as interpreter at 55 Rupees a month. I never saw anyone more upset than this man was when I told him this; hitherto he has looked very miserable and I imagined he would have jumped at the idea of not going on with me.

Mustafa Eff. left at 2 pm with a section of the 12th and about 130 donkeys accompanied by the Vet. Officer Salib Eff. Nushi Eff. and another section went with the party as additional escort till they are clear of the Boya.

6th April I let the sheep and goats taken by Bruce loose and they wandered off at once to the hills — about 30 had been taken for rations. Nushi Effendi returned about 11 am; the party had made about 10 miles the previous day and Nushi Eff. had waited till 8 am to safeguard the rear of the convoy. We started at 3 pm, our hamla reduced to about 170 donkeys and the whole force consequently much more compact. We kept outside the belt of thick bush which surrounds the hills, for the first 3 miles but then turned east and the going became rather difficult. Halted after 6½ miles to zeriba for the night.

7th April Started about 5.15. Lokitari the Dabosa boy led the way under escort, but became rather uncertain as to the way. Powell had a shot at a good bull eland which had two cows with them. After about 8 miles, we saw some people running away and after a little, when I was turning north to follow cattle tracks which must lead to the water, a woman was discovered hiding in the top of a tree.

Considerable persuasion brought her down and she soon became cheery and led us on our way. Seeing numbers of cattle in the distance soon after, I sent her on to say what charming people we were. Going on, I saw some men advancing slowly in the open forest, so in order not to frighten them, I went on with the interpreters and six men. The Dabosans declined to come right out to meet me and I had to advance further than was wise. The spokesmen were four or five elders and all the time I was talking to them, I could see numbers of the young men amongst the trees about 150 yards further on, perhaps a couple of hundred in all. The spokesmen went back twice to report our conversation; the upshot of it was that I convinced the older men that our intentions were peaceful but the younger men refused to let us go to the water, the elders offering to take me to another water further south. I did not at all like the look of things towards the latter part of the long palaver, the numbers in front were increasing and parties could be seen amongst the trees on either flank. I could not draw back in the middle of the talk without spoiling the whole affair and I fear my chances would have been small if the warriors had attacked me for I could not have been supported in time from the main body who were

4 or 500 yards away. Moreover such support would have weakened the guard for the hamla. I did not realise at the time that I was doing such an unwise thing. I sent back Adam to Harman to tell him to send some men off to the flank where I could see most of the warriors. Finally the old men came back and reported that they could not persuade the young ones, so I said that I was going to the water, that I did not want war but if anyone tried to attack, it would be war. I then went back to the main body and had it formed into [a] square, in which we advanced. As we approached the place of the palaver, I thought they would show fight but they gradually retreated. We walked on top of the wells almost at once, at least twenty about 12 feet deep with plentiful and good water. I paraded the square over all the ground where the natives had been gathered and then halted in an extended square, the people still hanging about in bunches in the trees. Throughout the warriors had been going through the usual warlike pantomime of beating the attack, striking their shields and shaking their spears. After we had been in camp about ¼ hour, I was told that some natives had come up and wanted to talk to me. I went out and met three old men one of whom was amongst the spokesmen of earlier in the day.

I now had a very long and rather amusing palaver. I was told by them that they had had to do with Swahilis who had robbed and attacked them but who were finally wiped out to a man. The beginning of the talk was really most amusing, the object clearly was to impress me with the power and invincibility of the Dabosa and to give way only step by step. At first they said that they had had scouts out who had given the news of our attack on Boya and that now messengers had been sent out to all the Dabosa gathering the clans to make war on us. They then said we might go through the country without delaying on the way. After much talk, illustrated by parables, I hope I managed to convey my meaning and intentions to them; making it clear that I did not want war but that if they did not supply our wants or if they attempted to molest us, it would be war. I told them to send out messengers in all directions to this affect and drew their particular attention to what happened at Boya to people who refused to sell what I wanted. The talk ended most satisfactorily by the men taking up earth, spitting on it and throwing it at me, and by their doing a sort of sword dance step over a bit of stick. I was interested by the form of swearing, one man taking hold of the nipple of his breast while swearing friendship. During the afternoon, the natives did not take advantage of my offer to let them water their cattle at the wells, but women and children came down quite fearlessly to draw water and quite a number of natives came into camp. Nothing was brought for sale though requests for wire and spearheads were many. Not an easy people to deal with but it is difficult to establish confidence in one day and I think we did well for the time being. I did not make a formal request for any supplies as I did not want to ask for anything which I could not immediately insist on getting or was prepared to take if necessary. I do not intend to take anything by force till I really want it.

We moved into zeriba for the evening, as I thought it well to stop here a little longer to establish confidence.

8th April   We left at 5.50 am and after a couple of miles crossed a khor at a point where it was dying away. Higher up this proved to be quite an important watercourse — the Lochoreatom. When we crossed it again a mile or so further up it was 70′ wide with 5′ banks. On the west side was forest with large trees, on the east 400′ of bush, then bare open plain. The idiosyncrasies of these watercourses are most peculiar. We passed some disused wells about 2½ miles and from what we heard after, there must be some open wells near there. Where we crossed the khor eventually there were a couple of deserted villages outside the forest.

We turned S.S.W. along the edge of the forest to the east side and eventually halted after 6½ miles total at a couple of disused wells sunk in a 'fula'. I had shot a tiang on the way and at the halting place went after a large herd of which I shot another one. Some natives came up when we halted, and some brought a tusk of about 60 lbs weight for sale. I went to some trouble to explain that we were not traders but that when the Government came permanently it would bring traders who would buy ivory and sell all sorts of luxuries. I had a long stalk after some Grant's gazelle before starting and eventually got a good one. The camel corps worked hard on opening up the wells, they gave a great deal of trouble by continually falling in, the understratum of sand being washed away by a strong rush of water.

I got one of the natives to show us the way to the next water Lobili-kuret, there proved to be a well worn path. We only did 3½ miles in the afternoon as we could not start till 4, owing to the slow rate of watering the donkeys. I let the guide go with a present of beads in the evening as he was afraid of the consequences if he went on with us to the village, the people of which would be angry with him for shewing us the way to them. Four men who had been following parallel to our route, came in to pay us a visit before dark. The attitude of the people is peculiar; they shew confidence but are not in the least inclined to bring in any supplies. I learnt from the guide the whereabouts of Muthing or Muzing from whose people Owen took the two cows last year and I explained to him that in fulfilment of Owen's promise I was going to restore the cows now. On the other hand I explained that if anyone refused to supply what I wanted, I would take it by force and *not* pay. I hope the news of our methods will spread, I think it will, for the people we saw today came from some distance and had come in to see us in a friendly manner after what they had heard.

9th April After a couple of miles we approached a khor with green trees and saw a number of spearmen lurking in front. Two men who apparently had followed us from yesterday at a distance eventually came up and made peace for us and we then went down together to the 6 wells of Lobilikuret about 30' deep with plenty of water. The people were quite anxious for us to stop but after filling the men's water bottles we went on. As Lokolan was said to be some distance south, I decided to go on to the Zangaiyetta said to be near. It appears that Lachokei and Lokolan are names derived from trees and are therefore common. There are moreover two Tuliabong's one at Lawurien which is probably on the upper water of the Lochoreatom and the other, further north, on the Lachokei, where Owen *****. The people at Lobilikuret were most friendly and all accompanied us onwards. We passed two villages on leaving the belt of wood near the wells and then into open country with some bush. After about 5 miles we arrived at a ridge with signs of cultivation and very large villages, the largest I have seen. Numbers of people in all directions, friends from Lobilikuret sending out messengers everywhere to give news of our friendliness. We arrived on the Zangaiyetta after a total march of about 9½ miles, here a broad river bed of some 400' with 2' banks and sandy bed. There was at the place we halted a large pool in a backwater and some wells near about 15' deep. Numbers of people came down and after we had settled down, I summoned all the elders for a palaver which lasted a long time. I went through all the usual talk of which I am getting very tired and it was attentively received. They told us that Darley whom they call Akanakileng had warned them that the Government was coming eventually and had told them to do what they were told and to not to attempt to fight. One man, a chief in his way, Lokatuka, produced a letter from Darley to say he was an honest, dependable man and that he had produced the murderer of one of Darley's men without urging. They spoke of Darley in quite a respectful way and there can be no doubt that he acted fairly to the Government and to them. They said they had very little grain but that they would try and bring some for sale.

I kept the chief and one of the elders with me but only a very little dhurra was brought in, about 50 rotls. As however I still have 5 days supplies, I decided to go without waiting for more grain. I let Lokitari alias Mordkin loose with a present of iron wire, he yammered for a spear head but I told him he had blotted his copy book by trying to escape. This he now says was because he thought I was trying to take him to Khartoum. His home, Nologir, is apparently about 3 hours south of our halting place (Loming). I had to take the chief and his adviser with us as guides as everyone else had disappeared. They became very restless after a short distance but I kept them till the chief's son arrived. The latter had gone off to send a message to Muzing to tell him I have two cows to repay those taken by Owen last year. This by the way seemed to make more impression than any of the rest of my talk. They had all professed themselves very pleased with the latter but I fear that the extreme friendliness and anxiety to please only lasts so long as they are not called upon to do any service. We started at 3 pm down the khor bed but we left after 2 miles, cutting through bush on the right bank and reaching the river again after 5½ miles. Here we found a village and a number of wells about 15′ deep in the river bed. They were nearly all dry and I thought they had been purposely filled in to prevent us drinking. However, I went down to the wells to see the people and went round and disarmed them all of their spears without any resistance on their part and then urged them to dig for water. It proved that the wells were really dry and digging down to clay brought no water except in two or three wells, so I eventually brought them to the zeriba and restored the spears. The son of the chief from the midday halt and his three friends stay with us, the former says he was with Darley when he came to Loggire and seems an intelligent and well meaning youth. I brought off a great piece of 'swank' this morning by shooting a gazelle at about 200 yards when we were being escorted by our body guard from Lobilikuret. This guard I should say was strengthened throughout by quite a considerable flank guard on either side who presumably were intended to give notice of any move on our part to intercept their cattle. We saw a few cattle and at the village by our night halt some sheep; this is

PLATE 17

The Madial–Tereteinia road

PLATE 18

Gerazmak Mukurio and some of his force at Bale. This incident took place some time in June, and does not feature in this diary, but it is of some significance. With the Commission completed, Kelly took a force towards the Abyssinian frontier, and is faced by a large force of armed men. As a result he returns to the British fort at Pibor (Plate 18).

PLATE 19

Entrance to Pibor fort.

PLATE 20

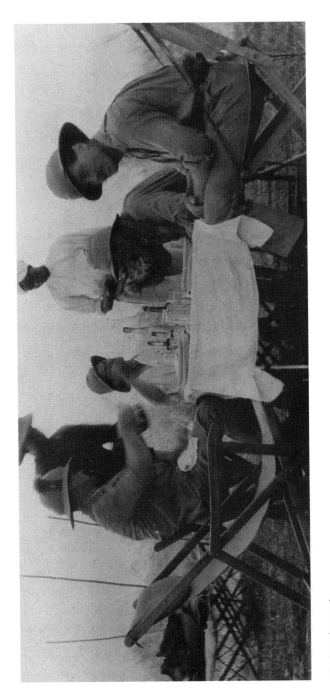

Lunch on the march.

quite a sign of confidence which was strengthened by the appearance of women and children at our midday halt. The chief's son says that the wells in the Zangaiyetta for about 7 hours down stream to Loko-sowen are all fallen in so tomorrow we should probably go east to Muzing's water the Murokawai and thence to the Lotilleit which is said to be nearly as big a river as the Zangaiyetta and not to lose itself as soon as the cotton. We crossed the Lotilleit apparently on our way from Kapedo to Kampi Morokko and it is fed by the Loyuru which we also crossed — called Laura by Darley.

10th April A late start owing to the bugler on duty oversleeping himself and the march was much delayed during the first three miles by the dense bush. We struck nearly east, leaving the Zangaiyetta for good and after 6 miles struck a large rocky khor with plenty of rain water, the Anakanaka coming from south, halting in an open spot soon after. On plotting out my map and questioning the guides, I have come to the conclusion that the Southern Column of the Beir Patrol was entirely deceived regarding the rivers, the Zangaiyetta is really the khor called Lachokei by them whereas the river they called the Z. is that which becomes the Lotilleit but which appears to be called Loka-lyan at first. Questioning the guides about the country ahead, I found that they know a good deal of the lie of the land beyond their own territory and I think we shall have no difficulty in getting to the Ji-e country with water all the way; I imagine the Lotilleit and Kuroni junction is vague in the dry season but is situated just about where I hope to strike the latter river.

I think that the sections of the Dabosa or Toposa as they really call themselves are (1) Musingo, the people of the Zangaiyetta (2) Loka-lyan, those of the Lokhalyan and Anakanaka (3) Magwois, those of the lower Lotilleit. Akara is I think merely the name by which the Latuka and Loggire call the Toposa. The cattle are now nearly all on the grazing grounds away from the main rivers — at Lowupo, Lochoreatom, Lokalan, Lawurien, Lobilkuret etc, the soil along the rivers being barren and bad grazing.

We started again at 3 and passing very numerous villages on our right hand on the bank of the Anakanaka, halted on a large river the Lokhalyan after 41¾ miles, about ¾ mile below the junction of the Anakanaka and Lokhalyan, which is called Murukwuri. We met on the way a son of Musing the chief from whom Owen took the cows[27] last year and sent him to tell Musing to come in to get his cows from us. We halted apparently in the very place where the Beir Patrol hit the river last year, coming due east from the Zangaiyetta. Musing, an old man nearly blind arrived before sunset and I gave him and the assembled people a long talk. I handed over two cows and a bull calf, the other cow is also said to be in calf. They seemed to be much impressed by getting this belated payment and welcomed the idea of the Government coming to settle down; Musing promised quantities of dhurra before 7 am and altogether the palaver was apparently most successful. They complained that the two guides whom Owen took last year never got any payment and I was able to tell them that the guides ran away without waiting to be paid. I have already promised Lomwuti, the son of Loratuka, an intelligent youth who went with Darley to Loggire and who seems very anxious to do his best, that he will get a cow if he takes us to the end of the Toposa country and brings Harman back. If he keeps to this bargain, it relieves me of some anxiety, as I was feeling a little doubtful about asking Harman to go back without guide or interpreter.

11th April Numbers of natives arrived early and two 'garrah's' of dhurra were produced. Much talk and haggling, and of course they asked for the things we have not got 'malods' and axes. I finally paid them well in brass and iron wire for what they brought, and I warned them and sent to tell Musing that if sufficient dhurra was not produced on payment by 11 am, I would send soldiers to the village to take it. They are undoubtedly most difficult people to deal with — grasping and suspicious; one would have thought the paying back of cows would have so impressed them that they would be anxious to bring in grain, more especially as they have heard what happened to Boya.

Finally, by 11 am about 300 rotls had been brought in all from the villages alongside our camp. I had sent again to Musing who replied that he had no dhurra. About 11.30 I started with Harman, Bruce and 10 men for the villages further south who had brought in no dhurra. We reached them after about ¾ mile, found them deserted though some natives were seen watching us. In three small villages we found nearly 3000 rotls of which we took about 900, leaving the remainder

[27] This incident with the cows was presumably during one of the Northern Patrols in 1912, which Owen accompanied as Medical Officer.

with the skins etc and iron wire in payment. Two of the owners eventually came up and I took pains to explain to them that as they had
been told to bring in grain and had not done so, I had now taken it
but was paying for it. I warned them that in future, if they did not
supply demands of the Government in the matter of grain, they would
not be so generously dealt with. When we reached camp, we found
Powell had sold some doses of quinine for a few garrahs of dhurra but
that no more had been brought.

At 2.30 pm, Bruce went with a weak section of the 12th to get
grain from Musing's villages, taking iron wire with him. We started at
3 pm, unfortunately without our guides who had disappeared. After
about a mile I had a note sent back by Bruce to say the people were
truculent. When I arrived at the village where he was, he said the
people had been very threatening. I found a few natives in the village
but they made no signs of making trouble. Huddleston and I then went
off to search another village which we found empty of grain. The
people had apparently removed it as Bruce had seen numbers of them
carrying loads away. I told Bruce to go on to the next village where
Bilel Effendi and his section were. When I got there, I heard shots and
met Bruce coming out to meet me to say that the people were threatening. Going up to the place where the shots were fired, I found Onbashi
Rahma Nur of the 12th in extremis with a spear wound through the
chest, a native with the top of his head blown off, another native 100
yards away dead and, I am sorry to say, a woman also dead. Bruce
had found a man inside one of the compounds, very threatening,
so had left the Onbashi with 3 men to watch the place while he himself
returned to tell me. The men's story was that the Onbashi was speared
by the man and that they had then shot his assailant and the man who
made to attack the sentry from outside.

We shall perhaps hear more accurate details after the Court of
Enquiry has sat tomorrow. At present one can only say that the incident
was most unfortunate and would apparently have been avoided if the
men had not been separated and had not, when left by themselves,
tried to tackle a cornered man. We halted near the place as the Onbashi
was still breathing but he soon died.

Having searched the group of villages thoroughly, we found about
2000 rotls of dhurra all of which I took and then burnt the villages.
The Onbashi was buried near. I regret the whole business intensely,
all our endeavours to get on friendly terms are now frustrated and
though I do not anticipate that the Dabosans will unite to attack us,

there will be no more friendly palavers or guides available either for our forward march now or for Harman's return journey. The best thing in the long run that could happen would be for them to attack in force and be severely defeated. Never till they have been thoroughly beaten, will they ever understand that the Government is and must be 'top dog'. Here of all places we might have expected to be well treated after our having given back the cows and had the long palavers yesterday. They have not the excuse that grain is scarce for we have seen very large areas cleared for cultivation.

12th April   We were roused about 1.30 am by numbers of natives with horns and shouts round the zeriba. The guard turned out but none of the natives came near and the noise quieted down when they found we were ready for them. We started at the usual time and had a rather trying march through thick bush. We passed several villages and were followed all the time by numbers of 'abied' yelling and yapping like a pack of curs.

I stopped twice at villages to talk to the people lurking behind the huts. I told them that I have no quarrel with the Dabosans except with the village who behaved badly yesterday, that I had been prepared to pay for dhurra, etc etc. They answered with a good deal of abuse, and the gist of the reply was that they did not want peace.

The last part of the march we did along the river bed of the Lokhalyan or Lotilleit and were fortunate after 9½ miles in finding water holes filled in which on being opened gave plenty of water at 3' depth. A picket was placed on the water and outposts all round the camp which was pitched in a cultivation zeriba where there was a little grass. Large numbers of natives collected in the bushes near the water and I told them several times that if they wanted peace they could have it but that if not, they must keep away or they would be shot at. They replied that they did not want peace, that they would die today, that they would wipe us all out in three days, that the fire of the burning villages would collect the whole Dabosa tribe to attack us. I left Lukuda with the water picket; the orders given to the NCOs in charge were that if any natives came within a circle of about 50 yards of them, Lukuda was to tell them twice to retire and if they did not do so, the soldiers were to shoot. About 1 pm, after the yelling had gone on continuously, we heard a shot and going to the picket, I found that one of the natives who had been warned repeatedly had been shot at and wounded. It appeared afterwards that this man who had been creeping up to attack when shot, was killed dead and was dragged away by his friends. This act may seem drastic, but there is no question that with such enormous numbers against us, the only way to keep the natives at a distance is to shoot straight when they overstep the limits. All possibility of friendly relations are, I fear, at an end and all we can do is to establish a funk.

A camel corps party going down to get water from another hole exercised great forbearance in not firing on natives who came near and actually withdrew. Last night I got Harman to put in orders that while regretting to announce the death of the Onbashi, I did not wish to give up hopes of getting on friendly terms with the Dabosa, that no firing was to be indulged in and if firing was ordered, strict fire control was to be observed. It is however incontestable that the Sudanese soldier gets 'bullet fever' and longs to let off his rifle on the smallest pretext. We went on at 3 pm, the animals slightly refreshed by the first feed of grass they have had since leaving Boya. Through thick low bush, we hit the Lotilleit after about 3 miles where it touches a group of low hills. Entering the river bed here, we saw numbers of natives who had been dogging our march throughout in the bed, rapidly making off under cover as we appeared. A mile's march along the river bed which shewed no signs of water, our unwanted escort still continuing their very unmusical cries. I was then told by the Shawish of the flank guard that he had passed a large 'fula' of water. I returned to this (on the left bank) and found a good camping place close to a fine pool of rain water; a good crop of grass here and the animals had a good hour's grazing before dark. The Court of Enquiry on the Onbashi's death with Powell as president, Huddleston and Nushi Effendi as Members sat today and found that the occurrence was due actually to disobedience of orders, in the Onbashi and men trying to take action in Bruce's absence.[28]

---

[28] Kelly's diary ends abruptly on the final sheet of his 104 page army-issue foolscap notebook. The story of the final days of his expedition after 12th April were almost certainly recorded in another notebook which has never been found.

Appendix 1

Recommendation of Commission on Soudan–Uganda Boundary Rectification

The boundary recommended by the Commissioners is as follows:

West Bank of the Bahr el Jebel

From a point on the bank of the river opposite the Unyami river, the riverain strip to the foothills of the escarpment as far as the mouth of the Khor Kayu (or Aju) to fall to the Soudan. The boundary to run up the Kayu from its mouth to the Khor Nyaura (?) thence up the latter khor to its source. From here to a point on the river Kaiya to be determined and then up the Kaiya to the Congo watershed. This recommended boundary will require verification and adjustment on the spot, the points aimed at being that the riverain people should fall to Soudan which will also take Kajo-Kaji and the Kuku tribe.

East of the Bahr el Jebel

The boundary will follow up the Unyama river from its mouth a distance of some ten miles to Jebel Ebijo, from the top of this hill a line towards Jebel Kadomera (the westernmost of the Amoji group of hill) to a point on the Assua river west of this hill, thence follow down the Assua river to Lokai — in order that a point on the Bahr el Jebel accessible to steamers may be secured to the Soudan, an enclave on the East bank above the Unyama river, a thousand yards by a thousand yards should be given to the Soudan. From Lokai the line to runs approximately north-east through uninhabited country to Jebel Matokko (Batogo or Atoko), this hill falling to Uganda. From Matokko a line running nearly due east to the summit of Jebel Agu, leaving the Farajok district to the Soudan and crossing the Farajok-Lukung road near a small hill two thousand yards south-east of the crossing of Khor Lapara. From Agu, a line to the highest point of Mount Alali and thence to the south peak of Mount Langia, leaving to Uganda the

Acholi on the south and south eastern slopes of the range: hence by
the small peak of Mount Tiya to the extreme north of Mount Teretania,
leaving the latter hill to Uganda, the line then runs approximately east
to the small hill called in Sheet I. 'Uganda' August 1900 Latome,
leaving the Logire Mountain and its southern continuation Mount
Momoi to the Soudan. From Latome, the line to run south of
Mount Harogo (the southern limit of the Dodinga tribe) and thence
eastward to the north of Mount Mogila (appr. Lat. 4°15′N and Long.
34°30′E). From here a theoretical line to the North of Mount Lubur
on Lake Rudolf is assumed, but if the northern portion of the lake
proves to be navigable, a strip of territory should be reserved to the
Soudan, affording a port on the lake. East of Mount Harogo, it has
proved impossible for the joint Commission to investigate owing to
the unfavourable season and the lack of water supply. Between this
mountain, therefore, and the lake the exact limits remain for further
consideration when the limits of the Turrana and Dabosa grazing
grounds are more accurately known.

The Commissioners recognise that owing to the inter-mixture of
the various tribes, it is impossible to determine a hard and fast tribal
boundary and suggest that when the territory on either side of the
frontier comes to be closely administered, any small alterations which
will facilitate administration can be effected.

(signed) H. H. Kelly. Captain R. E.
(Kaimakam, Egyptian Army)

H. M. Tufnell

(FO 407/177 f. 19488, 5 May 1913 (Public Records Office))

Madial
17–2–13.
(Note by Captain Kelly 24 April 1913: For Harogo,
Lotuke should be read. Latome is now fixed on map prepared.)
(From Sudan Archive, Durham, 186/1/297–298 Wingate Collection)

Appendix 2

Sudan–Uganda Boundary Rectification Notes Regarding Proposed Boundary Line

West Bank of Bahr el Jebel

The boundary recommended is not based on first hand knowledge on the part of either Commissioners and the main principles, namely, the inclusion of the Kaju-Kaji district and the Kuku and Bari tribes in the Sudan, being agreed upon, it should remain with the officials conversant with actual local conditions to arrange the exact line which will most conveniently separate the mixed population near the upper course of the Kaia river, and the Sudan Madi from those falling to Uganda. The transplanting of a few villages may prove desirable in order to make a thoroughly satisfactory boundary.

East Bank of Bahr el Jebel

Had it not been for the necessity of including Nimule in Sudan territory, the Uma river would have formed a perfect boundary as it is that already existing between the Bari and Madi. As it is, however, a considerable number of Madi must go to the Sudan and the boundary recommended will allow of an adequate supply of labour and grain to a Sudan post established at Nimule. Owing to the fact that no unity exists among the various sections of the Madi tribe, no great difficulty need be anticipated in their administration under two governments. The clause in the Commissioners' recommendations regarding a Sudan 'Enclave' to the south of the Nile-Unyama junction was inserted in order that direct access to the accostage point of steamers from the lake may be secured. Steamers now tie up south of the junction owing to difficulties in navigation down stream, and goods are lightered to Nimule (the present post being situated nearly a mile inland from the junction). The question of a site for a Sudan post will be discussed later in this report.

East of Lokai on the Assua river, the Acholi country is entered. This tribe causes some little difficulty as its limits are vague and off-shoots speaking a language identical or similar are widespread. The people of Farajok and Obbo for example are pure Acholi in language, type and origin, and should, therefore, properly speaking, go to Uganda. As, however, these districts have been entirely distinct under the existing administration from the Acholi proper, as they are separated from the latter by an uninhabited zone and as, finally, no more suitable dividing line could be found, it was considered that they would best fall to the Sudan, as being within easy reach of Nimule while distant from the administrative centre of the Acholi.

The so-called Agoro mountains are sparsely inhabited by a mixed population, only the southern and south eastern slopes have hitherto been administered and it is possibly here only in the whole range that pure Acholi are found. On the lower slopes on the east side are Latuka villages while the Abili, Mokuro and neighbouring hills are also inhabited by Latuka speaking people, and the Aiyerri near the head waters of the Gomorro or Kit river and the people of Tingali are believed to be of Latuka origin. Little is known of the inhabitants of the higher ground but they are probably for the most part of similar extraction to the Dongatolo of the Loggire hills who speak a Lango language midway between Latuka and Acholi. (It may be noted here that properly speaking, Lango is not the name of a tribe or race but it is the term applied by the Acholi to the hill-dwellers as a whole.)

The boundary recommended gives to Uganda all the administered Acholi and these are, as far as could be ascertained, all the people who can be looked upon as true Acholi; the few Acholi speaking hill people are distinct in habits and recent traditions. Lomorro, the late chief of Tarangole exercised considerable authority over the hill people to the north and north east and altogether the non-Acholi may be considered akin to the Latuka.

The Loggire group of hills is inhabited by two distinct peoples — the Dongatolo who occupy the higher ground, and the Loggire who live on the lower slopes; the latter are Lango and the former akin to Latuka. Apart from geographical considerations, the group falls naturally within Sudan territory as many of the Loggire owe allegiance to Ibrahim, the Latuka Chief of Lopi.

Tereteinia is mostly inhabited by Lango with a small proportion of true Acholi; with the exception of relations between the latter and Lumoi's people at Agoro, there is little connection with other hills; it has been on the main Uganda route eastwards since the administration has been pushed to the north and its inclusion in Uganda territory is recommended so that there may be no break in the continuity of administration. The inhabitants of the Loruwama group of hills (with Madial at its northern end) are for the most part Lango akin to Acholi, and though there is, on its north eastern slopes, a section akin to the Dodinga, geographically this group naturally falls to Uganda and existing difficulties occasioned by the close relations of a portion of it with the Dodinga can be dealt with administratively later.

The Kideppo valley crossed by the proposed boundary is uninhabited and the line cuts the continuation of the Dodinga range south of the prominent hill Lotuke (Harogo on existing maps) which is now uninhabited owing to inter-tribal disturbances. The stretch of low hills between Lotuke and Morongole is, as far as is known, uninhabited; or inhabited, if at all, by a few Wanderobo or cave dwellers.

Continuing east of Lotuke, the line runs to the north of Jebel Zulia, still through uninhabited country and thence to the north of Jebel Mogila. Until recently the Dabosa or Tabosa tribe went as far south as Zulia and eastwards as far as Lolimi, and they still claim as far as Mogila for their grazing and hunting grounds; they have however been ousted by the Turkana, who, it appears, have in their time been driven from their grazing grounds to the north west of the Rudolf plain by Abyssinian raids.

On account of water difficulties, the country east of Loruwama had to be visited by the Sudan party alone, which was provided with camel transport; no Turkana were met with, but as far as is known, the line from the north of Mogila to the north of Jebel Lubur and thence to Sanderson Gulf on Lake Rudolf will clear all the grazing grounds formerly occupied by the nomads of this tribe.

The clause regarding a Sudan enclave south of the boundary on Lake Rudolf was inserted to provide for such contingencies as a Uganda railway extension via Mount Elgon to the lake, for the possibility of shallow draught navigation on the lake proving feasible, and for the possible discovery of marketable commodities in the country north west of the lake.

Speaking generally, east of Tereteinia, inter-tribal raids have, by depopulating the intermediate zones, created a natural boundary which is that proposed for adoption. It may be considered moreover that with the exception of the riverain districts, the territory falling to

Bibliography

Barber, J. P. (1965) 'The moving frontier of British imperialism in northern Uganda 1898–1919', *Uganda Journal*, 29, 27–43.

Barber, J. P. (1968) *Imperial Frontier*. East African Publishing House, Nairobi.

Blake, G. H. (1994) Captain Kelly and The Sudan–Uganda Boundary Commission of 1913 in C. H. Schofield and R. N. Schofield (eds) *The Middle East and North Africa*, World Boundaries Volume 2, Routledge, London, 184–196.

Bright, R. G. T. (1908) 'The Uganda-Congo boundary commission', *Geographical Journal*, 32, 488–493.

Brown, A. F. and R. E. Massey (1929) *Flora of the Sudan*. Thomas Murby, London.

Brownlie, I. (1979) *African Boundaries: A Legal and Diplomatic Encyclopaedia*, Royal Institute for International Affairs. Hurst and Co., London, 917–921, 1002–1010.

Christy, C. (1917) 'The Nile-Congo watershed', *Geographical Journal*, 50, 199–216.

Collins, R. O. (1962) 'Sudan–Uganda boundary rectification and the Sudanese occupation of Madial 1914', *Uganda Journal*, 26, 140–153.

Daly, M. W. (1986). *Empire on the Nile: the Anglo-Egyptian Sudan 1898–1934*, Cambridge University Press.

Delmé Radcliffe, C. (1947) 'Extracts from Lt. Col. Delmé-Radcliffe's typescript diary report on the delimitation of the Anglo-German boundary, Uganda, 1902–1904', *Uganda Journal*, 11, 9–29.

Hill, R. *A Biographical Dictionary of The Sudan*, Frank Cass, London, (2nd edn.) 1967.

McEwen, A. (1971). *International Boundaries of East Africa*, Oxford University Press, 129–134 and 257–264.

U.S. Department of State, The Geographer (1970). International Boundary Studies No. 104: *Sudan–Uganda*. Washington.

FO 407/177 f. 4351 Sir Reginald Wingate to Viscount Kitchener 21 October 1911 (Public Record Office).

FO 407/177 f. 4351 Viscount Kitchener to Sir Edward Grey 27 October 1911 (Public Record Office).

FO 407177 f. 16972 Mr. R. J. Jackson to Mr. Harcourt 14 March 1912 (Public Record Office).

FO 407/177 f. 25592 Sir R. Wingate to Viscount Kitchener 5 June 1912 (Public Record Office).

FO 407/177 f. 48758 Sir R. Wingate to Viscount Kitchener 5 November 1912 (Public Record Office).

FO 407/177 f. 2697 Mr Harcourt to Officer Administering the Government of the Uganda Protectorate 28 November 1912 (Public Record Office).

FO 407/177 f. 27350 Viscount Kitchener to Sir Edward Grey 16 June 1913 (Public Record Office).

FO 407/177 f. 19488 Sir Edward Grey to Viscount Kitchener 5 May 1913 (Public Record Office).

Sudan Archive, Durham 186/1/297–298 (Wingate Collection).
Sudan Archive, Durham 133/1/22 Diary (H. H. Kelly Collection).
Sudan Archive, Durham A63/29–36 Photograph Album (H. H. Kelly Collection).

Index

NOTE: **Chiefs, Mountains** (including Jebels and Hills) and **Rivers** (including Wadis and Khors) are grouped under these headings
Place names are in *italics*
All names are spelled as they appear in the original text, with alternative spellings appearing in the text in brackets
* Denotes unidentified British officer or official